BRINGING
MARVIN
HOME

Our Adoption Journey

KATIE WYROSDICK

genesis
PUBLISHING GROUP

Bringing Marvin Home

Published by:
Genesis Publishing Group
Bartlesville, OK 74006
genesis-group.net

Edited by Lynn Copeland

Cover, page design, and production by Genesis Group

Printed in the United States of America

ISBN 978-1-933591-37-7 (pbk.)
ISBN 978-1-933591-38-4 (e-book)

Note: Most names within the story have been changed to protect the identity of the individuals.

You can find more information about Katie Wyrosdick (pronounced "Röz-dick") or inquire about speaking engagements at *kgwyrosdick@gmail.com* or follow us on Facebook and Instagram at *@bringingmarvinhome*.

To Marvin:

I pray that this book will be a gift to you when you grow older. I pray that it comforts you to have your story written down and forever in print. Most of all, I pray that you see in these pages how much you are loved and cherished, M' Pitit Gason.

Contents

Introduction

This is the story of how the most precious Haitian boy became a member of our forever family, our son, and the gift we never knew we needed. As I am sure most adoptive parents would agree, an adopted child is just as much a gift to you as you are to them, if not more so. This is definitely true in our situation. As I wake up to the beautiful brown eyes of my now eleven-year-old son, and his pre-teen voice saying, "Hey, Mom!" (even though it is always the crack of dawn!), I am forever grateful for this journey. I know that sometimes adoption doesn't go as you planned, hoped, or prayed that it would. Sometimes you get to see your reward on this side of heaven, and other times we won't know the answer or the reason until we get to heaven. Was it easy? Absolutely not. Would we do it all again? In a heartbeat!

■ ■ ■ ■

Every adoption story is unique, so to tell you how our journey began let me start with our family background. My husband, Mike, and I met our freshman year of college at the University of Tennessee in 1988. We always say it is a good thing we did not begin dating until our senior year, because we both agree we would have never made it as a couple if we had started dating as freshmen. Our first official date was Halloween 1991, and we were inseparable from then on. By spring break we were engaged and planned to marry following our graduation in May 1993. Both of us were on the five-year graduation plan for different reasons, and our parents were adamant that we finish college before the wedding. With that accomplished, on May 22, 1993, in my hometown of Jacksonville, Florida, I walked down the aisle of St. Mark's Lutheran Church to the funniest man I had ever met. I should not have been surprised that when he knelt down during the ceremony, the soles of his shoes revealed "Help me!," courtesy of his groomsmen. Typical, since we were the first of all of our friends to get married. I was warmly welcomed into the Wyrosdick (pronounced Röz-dick) family and gained many family members who would grow near and dear to my heart as the years passed.

Exactly twelve months, two hours, and twelve minutes later, our first daughter, Kelsey, was born on our first wedding anniversary. She was twelve days early, and I learned it is never a good idea to cook a huge pot of pinto beans for dinner when you are approaching your due date! We were young and scared, but incredibly excited about this beautiful baby girl in our arms. We both commented that she had the most beautiful lips and was perfect in every way.

After Kelsey was born, during the following year, I finished my Master of Science degree in Civil Engineering. I was grateful and blessed to be able to spend most of the first year at home with her as I finished up my thesis, and Mike ventured into his first full-time job after college. As graduation approached, I was offered a job with the Federal Highway Administration in Atlanta, Georgia. We decided Mike would be a stay-at-home dad while I worked full-time. One thing about our marriage is, it has never been traditional. I was often the "fix-it" person around the house, and Mike had no problem doing the lion's share of childcare, grocery shopping, doctor appointments, and more. What a blessing to know Kelsey was in the best hands possible while I was at work each day.

Given that I had terrible morning sickness when I was pregnant with Kelsey, we waited over three years to try to get pregnant again. I was working full-time and needed Kelsey to be a little more self-sufficient in case I was really sick again. It is a good thing we waited, because my morning sickness was worse the second time around. I had intense nausea and vomiting for five months straight. Until you have experienced it, you can never truly appreciate not feeling nauseated all the time. When those days passed, I was one happy camper. Four years and five days after Kelsey was born, we welcomed Gwendolyn Brooke into the world. She was such a beautiful baby, with a head full of dark hair and striking blue eyes. She was the perfect second baby for us; she was very laid back and frequently slept through the night when just a few weeks old. We knew she was going to be a "mover and shaker" when she started crawling at four months, and, boy, were we right! We used to call her Houdini because she could escape anything we confined her to. Cribs, car seats, strollers, the church nursery…you name it, and she escaped it. Thank the Lord, she was never injured.

What a blessing to have two healthy, beautiful girls. Mike continued his stay-at-home duties, and three months after Brooke was born, I reluctantly headed back to work. I loved my job, but was miserable with the Atlanta commute, and felt like I was missing out on the formative years for the girls. I truly wanted to be a stay-at-home mom. After Brooke's first birthday (May 1999), we started putting plans in motion to move back to Knoxville, Tennessee.

In Atlanta, Mike had started up a part-time landscaping business. We knew he could not move the business to Knoxville and have enough initial customers to support our family. The plan was for Mike to find full-time work in sales and for me to stay at home with the girls. However, God had bigger and better plans. Within six months of our moving back, the company Mike was working for closed their Knoxville office. With lots of prayer, he took his severance package and, with help from family, started up our landscaping business. I say "our" because Mike quickly needed my help with the management of the business, and our business partnership was born. We've been working literally side by side (our desks almost touch each other) ever since, and thankfully, our opposite personality traits complement each other in most situations. While we have each "quit" or been "fired" a few times over the years, and, it is said, I may have tossed a box of crackers in his general direction, the partnership has been almost seamless!

In the early years of the business, I wanted to have a third child, but we were beyond busy with all that is involved in running a small business. To be honest, adoption had never really entered our discussions about having a third child, but I certainly was not opposed to the idea. As far as another biological child was concerned, I was afraid of what would happen if I had morning (all-day) sickness again for months with two young kids and a rapidly growing business. I prayed that, if it was not wise for us to have another child, the Lord would take away my desire, which at the time He did. So, our lives with the girls were filled with laughter, family, church, friends, sports, music, and much more over the years.

CHAPTER 1

Mission Trip Bound

*Religion that God our Father accepts as pure and faultless
is this: to look after orphans and widows in their distress
and to keep oneself from being polluted by the world.*
—JAMES 1:27

As our girls were growing up, 2012 may have been our
most eventful year up to that point. In the spring, we
were in the midst of Kelsey's senior year in high school, knee
deep in the final preparations for her upcoming university
experience. If you have been through this, you know it
involves a mountain of paperwork, meetings, college visits,
etc. Kelsey had narrowed her search to two small, Christian
universities but hadn't made her final decision. With Kelsey
being on her high school track team, we were busy with
sporting events on a weekly basis. Brooke was in her last year
of middle school and spending most of her free time playing
softball and taking piano lessons. As a family, we had discussed the possibility of going on a mission trip together,
and at age thirteen Brooke was finally old enough to attend
several of the mission trips that our church offered.

Carving out time from school, church, sports, and family
activities to go on any week-long trip is hard to do, but I
especially wanted our family to experience a mission trip

together before Kelsey went away to college. For several years, I had felt God tugging at my heart to participate in a life-changing mission trip. We weren't sure if we could financially swing a trip during this stage in our lives. We had just experienced another yearly loss (the third in a row) for our family business. The Great Recession had not been kind to our landscape business. We were very grateful to still be in business, but we were struggling to keep it profitable. We prayed about the financial means to go and if it was wise to utilize our depleted savings account.

Our church had been financially supporting two orphanages in Haiti for several years, providing funds for the children's food, housing, caregivers, and schooling. They had scheduled an upcoming mission trip to Haiti to visit the two orphanages. The trip would be composed mostly of youth group members, their families, and youth leaders. Even better, Kelsey's small group leader and her husband were leading the next trip to Haiti. They were a huge reason we chose this mission trip and felt comfortable with the team. They had been to Haiti before and had shared about their love for the country and especially the children who had stolen their hearts. After prayerfully considering the costs, we signed up for the trip, then started fundraising to help cover some of the costs to send four of us on the Haiti mission trip. We were all so excited about this opportunity to serve, love on some children, and experience our first international mission trip together. The idea of spending time with orphans in Haiti appealed to all of us. We had all served with the children's ministry in some capacity over the many years we had been involved with our churches. We were looking forward to serving the "least of these."

I immediately started my "super-planning mode," which, being the engineer that I am, naturally involved lots of list making. I was pumped up but a little scared as well. I am a bit of a germaphobe, and as a former transportation safety engineer, I had some fears about things that could go wrong in a third-world country. We were briefed during pre-trip meetings on what we could expect, what we might see or experience, and proper safety measures. The leaders did their best to prepare us for what we could encounter. We were told of the devastation we would see in the aftermath of the 2010 earthquake. We were warned of the dangers we could face. An armed guard had even angrily boarded the bus on a prior mission trip because a student had innocently taken a picture of him on the street. Thankfully, the translator on that trip was able to calm him down after the offending photos were deleted, and the group was able to safely move on their way. Within a few short weeks, with God and a hefty batch of antibacterial wipes, we were ready to go.

Katie's Facebook Entry: February 6, 2012

Had our first Haiti mission trip meeting yesterday. We are soooo excited about this trip! I can't wait to see how the Lord changes our hearts forever and for the opportunity to love on some orphans.

HEADING TO HAITI

On March 15, 2012, at the crack of dawn, twelve of us boarded a plane headed to Port-au-Prince via Miami, Florida. We had been blessed to travel to many foreign countries with Mike's family and on business reward trips, so I was not nervous about the process of getting to Haiti. However, I was nervous about what it would be like when we arrived. We had been forewarned by the team leaders about the Port-au-Prince airport. Since the earthquake in 2010, the airport had only makeshift repairs to get it back in operating condition, but it was less than ideal. It was quite chaotic, and *everyone* wanted to help you with your bag. If three men "helped" you with your bag, you were expected to tip all three of them. We were told not to let anyone help with our bags. When we finally arrived at the team bus, I refused to let the pastor of the Haitian partner church help me with my bag. Embarrassingly, I thought he was just another baggage handler.

After we loaded our minibus at the airport, we headed to the mission house. It was a bumpy, eye-opening ride. Having visited several other countries, Mike and I thought we were "prepared" for what we would see. If you have been to Haiti, you know what I mean. The 2010 earthquake devastated so much of the capitol city, and they were definitely still recovering from the extensive damage. There were still collapsed houses that made you wonder how many people had perished in that home. It was sobering, to say the least.

The guest house was a good-sized, two-story home with several bedrooms on the second floor. The guest house was run by Pastor Charles and his wife, who in my opinion, was one of the best cooks I've ever encountered. Since it served as a guest house for missionaries, the rooms had been divided into boys' and girls' rooms with bunk beds and other twin beds. The perimeter of the home was protected by a stone wall with broken glass at the top. Broken bottles had been cemented into the wall. There was a large metal gate that kept the property sealed off from the general public, and a private, armed security guard was on site at all times. All of these security measures offered a level of comfort I did not know I would need but was thankful for. Haiti is a very dangerous country and is often listed as a "do not travel" area by the United States government. This is mostly due to violent crime and kidnappings perpetrated on visitors and locals.

After getting settled into our dorm-like room at the guest house, we changed clothes and prepared to head to the first orphanage for the afternoon. The orphanages our church had sponsored following the earthquake were Delivrans Mwen, in a northern suburb of Port-au-Prince, and Foyer des Amis, in the neighboring suburb of Carrefour. The two orphanages were very different in the way in which they were run.

Delivrans Mwen was associated with the Delivrans Mwen church, led by Pastor Odson. It was run by Madame Berger and had children ranging in age from one to thirteen. Madame Berger ran a tight ship, and the kids were fairly clean and well behaved, but they were hungry for one-on-one attention. We gathered they had visitors about once a quarter, but we were not sure as to the frequency of missionary visits. We did find out later that other churches were also helping to support the orphanage. As you could imagine, it would be hard to "love on" two or three dozen children without the modern-day conveniences that we enjoy. Delivrans Mwen existed in a two-story home that no longer had electricity or running water. The wastewater plumbing was still functioning, so they flushed the toilets using a bucket of water from their cistern, an underground tank in the back yard of the property. Their cooking and bathing also took place here, in a concrete "yard" of sorts. The cooking was done on open fires, and the bathing consisted of small buckets of cold water dumped over the children, using water fetched from the cistern.

There appeared to be about three helpers in addition to Madame Berger. We found out later that the children were eating only one proper meal a day. That meal consisted of rice and a few beans, cooked in huge pots out back. All the children sat on wooden benches with a taller wooden bench serving as a table to eat from. Even the smallest of children were adept at eating that plate of rice and beans without spilling a morsel, skillfully balancing their food on a twelve-inch-wide piece of wood. Most of the plates were upside down frisbees but some were real plates. They had only water to drink. Aside from the meager beans, very little, if any, protein was served with their meals.

Marvin eating on a frisbee

Foyer des Amis contained a much wider age range of children, with some of the children already aging out of the home. Once children reached age eighteen, they would be forced to leave, as the orphanage could no longer afford to care for them. I am sure most were terrified of finding themselves as adults alone on the street, looking for any meager way to survive. The children at this orphanage were visibly dirtier, many with advanced tooth decay, and the younger children were not as willing to connect with the team one-on-one. They seemed more distant and resigned to life as orphans. It was obvious they were more self-governed and that had obviously been detrimental to their development.

On the day we arrived in Haiti, we only had time to spend the afternoon at Delivrans Mwen. We all ended up in the back "play yard," which was just a narrow, sloped concrete area behind the house. That first day was such a blur, I did not even remember the precious little boy sitting next to me while I had two girls sitting on my lap. As I looked back on the pictures from the day, I realized that our future son, Marvin, was sitting right beside me. All of the children just wanted to be close to us and touching us at all times. They did not care that it was 98 degrees outside and we were all sweating profusely.

Our first encounter: Marvin to my right,
sitting on the ground

We spent several hours with the children, teaching them some of the games and crafts we brought with us. Time went by fast, and it was exciting to watch our girls in this mission environment. Brooke immediately bonded with a spunky little girl named Jacqueline; Kelsey became "the baby whisperer," quickly lulling any little ones to sleep in her arms; Mike bonded with a troubled little girl named Fofaline; and I latched on to Jacqueline's older sister, Sofiani. As the hours wore on, we realized that our visit was a welcome break in the monotony of orphanage living, especially in an orphanage where there was never enough money—and therefore food—to last through the month. We ended the first day wondering what it would be like to be so starved for adequate nutrition, and, maybe more importantly, for love and affection. When we arrived back at the mission house for our first Haitian meal, we had some time to discuss the events of the day. All of the first timers were still processing what they had seen in the short six-hour period. Most people who experience Haiti are changed forever, and we were no exception to this God-movement in our lives.

SO MUCH TO PROCESS

The exhausted group took turns showering in a freezing-cold shower, but we were grateful after the extreme heat of the day. The water at the guest house, like most homes, is delivered weekly by the water truck. I am not sure if any homes have water supplied by any kind of utility infrastructure. These huge plastic water tanks sit on top of the roofs throughout the city. Every day you could hear the water truck playing its melodious song as it traveled down the streets of Port-au-Prince. It would stop and, using a long hose and some kind of pump, deliver gallons of water to the storage tank on each rooftop. Because water is not unlimited there, we were all very careful about the amount of water we used during showering. Basically, we would get wet, turn off the water, lather up with soap and shampoo, then turn the water back on to rinse as quickly as possible. This quick shower worked out well, since even though we had been sweating profusely all day long, a cold shower is hard to enjoy. After cleaning up, we all crashed in our sea of bunk beds, with boys in one room and girls in the other. Thankfully, the guest house had multiple floor fans and screens on the windows. Though it was hot and humid, I was able to fall asleep relatively quickly.

On the second day of our trip, we would visit Delivrans Mwen again in the morning and Foyer des Amis in the afternoon. When we arrived at Delivrans Mwen, we were ushered into one of the larger upstairs bedrooms to play with the

Marvin on our first visit

kids. The bedroom consisted of several metal bunk beds and a built-in armoire against the wall to the left of the door. When I walked in, Marvin toddled right up to me and put his little hands out for me to pick him up. Of course, I was happy to oblige, and he wrapped my neck in the biggest bear hug and would not let go. After he hugged my neck for what felt like an eternity, he laid his head on my shoulder and just rested there. Given that this was first thing in the morning, I knew he was probably not tired, but just really missed the loving touch of a parent or caregiver. Tears started streaming down my face. I wondered, who loves on this precious boy when visitors are not there? I felt an immediate attachment to this loving little one and questioned if that was possible. Some of the children were wondering why I was crying, and my girls and Mike gave me the "Oh, no!" look. Did I mention that I am a very emotional person? I am one of those people who cry over commercials!

Marvin looked to be about eighteen months old and appeared to be a little under the weather with a runny nose. His toes hung off the edge of his too-small shoes. His hair was shaved short but was solid black, which was a good sign that he was not iron deficient. (We found out later that some of the little ones with reddish hair were deficient in iron, and that was why their black hair had turned red.) He had a beautiful smile, chubby little hands, and a loving disposition.

Throughout our visits to his orphanage each day, Marvin took turns sleeping in each of our laps and was never far from our arms. This boy loved to sleep, eat, and kick a ball. Anytime we provided snacks for the children, I could tell they were very hungry, and Marvin was no exception. He would absolutely devour any snack we provided and be looking for more. This was a reality I knew we would face, but I do not think you can adequately prepare for the expression in a hungry child's eyes. They looked to us to make it better and alleviate their pain. Those were some of the most devastating feelings of pain and guilt I had ever experienced.

We spent the remainder of our days playing and loving on the children at both orphanages. We were able to enjoy a moving church service, even though it was in Haitian Creole. We came to know and love the small circle of Haitian friends we had met during this quick visit. Haiti has a way of stealing a piece of your heart every time you visit.

ALREADY FALLING IN LOVE

It was becoming obvious that our whole family was absolutely falling in love with Marvin. We connected with many of the other children, but this connection with Marvin seemed to be different. The amazing thing was, we all felt this same bond with him. Even as a little toddler, he had the most amazing disposition. On the last day, we picked up Marvin, and all four of us gathered around for a photo with

Our first "family portrait" in Haiti, March 2012

him. While taking the picture, Mike chimed in, "Family portrait," and my heart just about skipped a beat.

Thoughts started swirling through my head. Would Mike really consider adopting this precious child we had come to love in such a short time? We all laughed and pondered how we could make Marvin a part of our forever family. Brooke and our Haitian translator, Peterson, were determined that we could "just bring him home." I assured Peterson and Brooke that I did not want to end up in a Haiti prison cell for the rest of my life. Both girls were determined that Marvin would be their brother and that we were going to adopt him. We promised the girls we would talk and pray about it when we got home. I also couldn't help remembering the possibly "prophetic" words of Mike's sister, Buffy, before we left on our trip. She had hugged us goodbye and said, "Now go meet my little nephew!" Somehow, after the news coverage of the 2010 earthquake, Buffy felt in her heart we would someday adopt from Haiti.

Mike and I had never shared a desire to adopt with anyone that we could remember. We did not go on the mission trip to Haiti with the intention to adopt. I guess you could say we have always had open hearts and an open home. Over the years, we have had several people live with us during their time of need and, as small business owners, we had taken many people "under our wings." I suppose those things may have led Buffy to believe we would be open to welcoming a precious son in need of a forever family.

On the last day, we said our goodbyes and boarded the bus to leave. I sobbed a good portion of the way back to the guest house. I truly felt physical pain leaving the orphanage. My heart was breaking already for Marvin and all the precious children we had connected with who had no family.

Sometimes the hurts of this world are just too much to bear, and I needed a good cry in the arms of my heavenly Father.

Kelsey the "Baby Whisperer" with Marvin

Brooke and Jaqueline

CHAPTER 2

Forever Changed

If I give all I possess to the poor and give over my body to hardship that I may boast, but do not have love, I gain nothing.

—1 CORINTHIANS 13:3

We returned home exhausted and ready for a long, hot shower. I have to say, that was really the only thing I missed while on our trip (and maybe being able to rinse my toothbrush under running water). It was exciting to visit with Mike's parents, Sharon and Jay, and sister, Buffy, who live nearby, and tell them all about our trip and especially about Marvin. Buffy may have snuck in an "I told you so" as we were sharing all the details of our trip and about the precious little boy we bonded with.

As promised, within a week of our return Mike and I had talked and prayed about adopting Marvin. We considered our ages, and the fact that we would be starting all over again in the parenting department. In a few short years we would be "empty nesters"; were we really ready to do this all over again, this time starting in our forties? Financially, were we even in a position to pursue this adoption? Would we, or the girls, someday regret adding to our family if Marvin turned out to be emotionally scarred and difficult to parent? Were we equipped to handle that scenario if that was our reality?

These were all scary, hard, and valid questions. In the end, though, it did not take long to make the decision that would ultimately change our family forever. We both felt like we were being led to pursue the adoption of Marvin, to make him a part of our forever family. The girls were in the kitchen when we delivered the news, and they both shouted for joy. Lord willing, they were going to have a brother someday. We just had no idea if it was even possible, or where to begin. But of course, all great undertakings nowadays must begin with an Internet search, and I began doing research on the possibility of adopting from Haiti.

Facebook Entry: March 30, 2012

Well, it's official. We are going to pursue adoption of Marvin. Our hearts are bursting with joy!!! Praying the Lord clears our path and we bring him home some day. Blessed beyond measure…

I remembered a conversation that I had with a friend on the mission trip. Shawn had been to Haiti many times on medical mission trips and had investigated adopting a precious boy named Wesley. After some time, he found out that Wesley was an economic orphan who had two living parents and a brother. His parents loved him enough to place him in an orphanage to preserve his life. Orphanages are often sponsored by churches, and it is a sad reality that an orphanage may be the only place children can receive a decent or life-sustaining amount of food and any level of education. Shawn decided it would be best to help Wesley's parents care for him and his brother, so the boys could remain in their home with their parents. In the process, though, he had made connections with a man from a Knoxville church who helped others adopt in Haiti.

Not knowing how to contact him directly, I contacted his church. Through their reply, I found out that he no longer attended their church or worked with their orphanage, but they put me in touch with a lady who still facilitated adoptions in Haiti. It turned out that in 2010, Lisa was in the process of adopting a little girl named Ashoni when the earthquake struck. Lisa had just left Port-au-Prince the day before the earthquake. Sadly, Ashoni was the only little girl from their orphanage, Chante Lajwa, who perished in the earthquake. After losing Ashoni, Lisa had dedicated her spare time (on top of raising two children and working full time) to helping families adopt children from their church-sponsored orphanage in Haiti.

One afternoon, I contacted Lisa and she was gracious enough to entertain a long conversation with me about the adoption process. As she threw out names of documents, processes, and facilitators, my head was swimming in details, and we agreed to meet soon for dinner. Shawn wanted to meet with all of us too, and so did another couple from our church who were interested in adopting. We had attended the mission trip with the wife of this family, and she was head over heels in love with a spunky, little girl named Ashlin with a mile-wide smile. The trip we were on together was her second trip, but her husband had not been able to visit Haiti yet and had not met Ashlin. They did not want to commit to pursuing the adoption of Ashlin until he had met her, but because of the strong possibility that they might adopt, they were very interested in hearing what Lisa had to say. We all enjoyed a nice dinner and soaked in as much information as we could from Lisa.

During these early conversations, we discovered Delivrans Mwen was not licensed to process adoptions, so we assumed our ultimate goal was to get them licensed and to have many of the children adopted through the partnership between the orphanage and our church. The process is long and difficult, so many orphanages do not pursue licensure. Shawn had already been working with Pastor Odson to obtain a crèche license for the orphanage, which is the first step in being able to process adoptions. We also learned from Lisa that we would need a Haitian lawyer as well as a Haitian facilitator in place who could work closely with the orphanage. These facilitators were very specialized and needed to be connected with the judicial system within the city in which they work.

We immediately realized this could be a very difficult person to find. We wondered if someone in Haiti could shadow Lisa's facilitator to "learn the ropes" before going out on their own, but who could that person be? Where could we find him or her? Neither Mike nor I really wanted to be a guinea pig in this process either, as we knew that could be costly in both time and money, and the adoption may not be successful after all that time and effort.

We left the meeting with Lisa with some detailed information on the process of adopting from Haiti. Lisa was generous and shared her paperwork steps that she gives to families adopting from their orphanage. After this meeting, Mike and I prayed, and we felt led to begin the process as if the crèche license, facilitator, and lawyer were already in place. We did not know how God was going to provide all that we needed, but we felt His leading that He would.

CHAPTER 3

Beginning the Process

I will praise the Lord, who counsels me; even at night my heart instructs me.
—PSALM 16:7

*W*e officially started adoption paperwork in April 2012. I began by gathering original documents for our entire family, such as our birth certificates (of course, we were all born in four different states) and marriage license. I contacted a Tennessee adoption agency that could perform our home study and scheduled it for late June. The home study required a significant gathering of information, and I knew I needed some extra time to be prepared. We were very busy with the last few months of school, and this season went by in such a blur.

May 20, 2012, was a special day for our family. Our eldest child ventured into the official world of "High School Graduate." Four years after Kelsey graduated fifth in her class, Brooke did the same thing. We might be a slightly competitive family. We always joked that the family "smarts" must have skipped a generation. We enjoyed celebrating with family who had joined us for the graduation. Somehow, we had successfully navigated kindergarten through twelfth grade, and it all seemed to happen in the blink of an eye.

As the summer entered full swing, we had heard rumblings that the adoption laws were about to change in Haiti. Apparently, for many years, Haiti leaders had been discussing adopting the Hague Convention. The Hague Convention had been adopted by many countries and had measures in place to prevent child trafficking. One of its measures included not being able to pre-select your child. In other words, you could not fall in love with a child and then decide you wanted to adopt them. While we understood the reasoning behind the measures, this made us very worried that we might never be able to adopt the son we had come to love. We were not sure how we were going to move forward without a Haitian facilitator in place, but now we could be faced with a hard and fast deadline to get our adoption paperwork submitted before the Hague Convention became law. If we did not get our documents submitted to Haiti prior to September 1, our possibility of bringing Marvin home would have been over. Thankfully, no obstacle was too great for our God, and we were really just along for the amazing ride!

Facebook Entry: June 17, 2012

So, please pray for the adoption process. It's a lot to explain on FB, but we may have a hard deadline of August 1st for everything to be in Haiti. This can be a huge blessing in disguise if the facilitator accepts our case & if we can get it all done. Many prayers needed so we can someday bring Marvin home…

After learning about the pending Hague Convention changes to the adoption law in Haiti, I received a phone call from Lisa in mid-June. She asked if we had heard about the possible law changes and inquired about how far along we were in the process. Thankfully, we had already started the home study process, and we had made good progress toward gathering the many documents required for the dossier. Lisa then told us that she and her organization were willing to take on our case, but only if we were far enough along in the process. Our family of four happened to be in the car when we received this news, and we were all very grateful for another open door in this journey! I was thankful we were all together to receive this incredible news. Sadly, I realized that the family who adored Ashlin would not be far enough along in the process. At the same time I felt immense joy at our news, I also felt grief for the loss of their opportunity to bring Ashlin home.

Shortly after the joy of securing a facilitator wore off, a little bit of panic set in as we realized how much paperwork had to be done by August. Our home study was not even scheduled until June 26. After the social worker visited the home and compiled all the documentation required, she would still have to complete her report, including reviews by a supervisor. I contacted the agency we were using, and they were gracious enough to say they would try their best to work with our fast-approaching deadline.

CHAPTER 4

A Sea of Paperwork

You need to persevere so that when you have done the
will of God, you will receive what he has promised.
—HEBREWS 10:36

*W*e picked up the pace and made plans to travel to
Nashville to get our important documents authenticated at the state level and for Mike and me to be fingerprinted. We secured a translator in California to translate all
our documents into French. We chose a translator located so
far away only because his services would fit within our dwindling budget, though it would present some hurdles further
down the road. I never thought the French I took in high
school would come in handy, but I smiled as I knew God had
planned this long ago. I was thankful for that experience as I
somewhat successfully reviewed all my French documents
for errors in names and dates.

I became very friendly with the local FedEx personnel, as
I sent documents all over the country. We participated in
home study interviews and psychological evaluations; gathered up recent tax returns, bank statements, letters of recom-
mendation, letters of employment, birth certificates, and
marriage certificates; secured powers of attorney; received
local criminal clearances; were fingerprinted in Nashville at

the Tennessee Bureau of Investigation, and more! Kelsey had to do her biometrics/fingerprinting in Birmingham, because she was already at college. The list seemed never ending, but one day it would all be worth it. I jokingly thought about how much harder this was than going to prenatal classes for my biological children. I also became well acquainted with the notary at my local bank, as almost every document had to be notarized. She could not wait to meet Marvin, asking for updates and photos of him every time I would go to the bank.

Once all the documents were gathered, I had to take every notarized document to our local county office where the notary stamp originated. Not realizing beforehand that I had three different counties represented in our paperwork, I had to visit three separate counties. The county had to certify that the notary's stamp was valid for each stamped document. Each county was a unique and interesting experience, to say the least. One county was closed on July 5 (apparently, they take the day off after the Fourth), so I had to repeat the twenty-mile trip the following day. Another county had an elderly employee who accidentally pulled the notary record for the wrong notary, which naturally required an additional trip back to the county office once I realized his mistake. This extra trip also happened to be on the same day as our trip to Nashville for authentication of the documents. At this point, I learned my lesson to not leave any government office without double-checking the document's information.

After obtaining county-level certification, we had to take all these documents and certifications to the state office to be authenticated. Authentication was basically the state acknowledging that the county notary stamps were valid. We lived in Knoxville, so we were required to travel almost three hours to Nashville to get our documents authenticated. On this trip to Nashville, we also picked up our home study results in person. Normally, you would wait for them to be mailed but since we were in a rush, we were able to skip the mailing process. While there, we had to have our home study certified as well, because the agency we used was from Nashville, which required a Davidson County stamp. About an hour and a half later, we left Nashville with a large stack of authenticated documents. During the authentication process, they stapled legal-sized, blue paper over the top edge of all our documents. Thankfully, I had been properly warned not to remove those staples for any reason or we would have to start the process all over again. Having your documents stapled together with a folded over piece of paper doesn't sound like a big deal—until you need to make three photocopies of every page and scan in each page of every authenticated set of documents, and you cannot take them apart!

Facebook entry: July 6, 2012:
On the way back from Nashville with 18 authenticated adoption documents! Making good progress, thank You, Lord!!

PAPERWORK FOR DAYS

After the state-level authentication, we had to have all these documents translated into French, including each notary stamp, certification, and authentication. I scanned eighty-one documents and sent them all by email to our translator in California. I had let him know in advance about our hard and fast deadline, and thankfully he was very accommodating and returned our translations as soon as possible. Within eight days, I received them back and began to check them for errors. I also had to print them all out and match them up with the appropriate English version of the documents. This step was extremely difficult and took several hours, but, again, I was thankful for the years of French I studied in high school.

Finally, the whole slew of documents had to be legalized by the Haitian Consulate in Chicago. I couriered all these documents overnight to Chicago, with a check to cover the cost of each document and a pre-paid overnight envelope for their return. Sure enough, in two days they were returned to us with a special stamp on the front. This was probably the fastest part of the entire process. If any of the documents were incorrect, they would just send them back in the package with no explanation as to why. This happened with my birth certificate and our translator's certification document. I was not sure why they had been returned to us unapproved, so I called the consulate to get clarification. It turned out that they wanted my birth certificate authenticated on the state level in Illinois, and the translator's certificate through California. It was not sufficient that they had original stamps on them. In the middle of all this paperwork, we thankfully received notification from the US Citizenship and Immigration Services (USCIS) that our petition to adopt internationally had been approved! This would be the first hurdle on the US side before we could adopt.

By this time, we were fast approaching the deadline for our paperwork to be in Haiti, and I was very nervous we were going to miss the deadline. I quickly overnighted the documents to Illinois and California, respectively, and anxiously awaited their return. My birth certificate from Illinois came back quickly, but the translator's certificate from California did not. I searched online for a phone number to call, but when I called, I could not get a live person on the phone for almost a week. Since the recession in 2008, the state had been operating under a major budget and personnel shortage. When I was finally able to reach a human being, I found out that they could not courier my document back, even though I included a prepaid envelope for them to do so. They said they were required to send it back to me by regular postal mail. My goodness, I could have screamed! In my opinion, this was the craziest thing I had ever heard.

The Lord was faithful, and the documents arrived in time for me to make three copies of everything. Now remember, I could not take any of the documents apart, so this meant at least two hours of photocopying, and another two hours of properly sorting the copies. I felt a huge sense of relief and satisfaction when it was all done and our paperwork was ready to be hand-delivered to Port-au-Prince, Haiti. Thankfully, a sweet couple also in the process of adopting took our dossier with them on their trip to Haiti and hand-delivered it to the facilitator.

Facebook Entry: August 26, 2012

Yes, this sea of adoption paperwork will all be in order tonight & ready to be hand-delivered to Haiti on Friday. Wish I could take it myself :-(I am thankful that I took French in high school (never, ever thought it would be of use)! Who knew?

CHAPTER 5

True Orphan?

"I will not leave you as orphans; I will come to you."
—JOHN 14:18

*B*efore all the paperwork was submitted to Haiti in late August, Mike, Brooke, and I traveled to Panama City Beach, Florida, with Brooke's travel softball team. We had a great time watching Brooke play softball and spending time at the beach. While we were in Florida, Lisa was conducting some adoption business in Haiti. Since they had agreed to take our case, her facilitator, Ricardo, needed to meet Marvin and the madame of the orphanage. We had been in touch with Pastor Odson to let him know of our intentions to adopt Marvin, and we had asked and received his permission to pursue the adoption. We had also previously emailed him to let him know that Ricardo was willing to be our facilitator, since Delivrans Mwen had not yet received their crèche license, and we were now looking at a hard and fast deadline to be able to adopt Marvin under the old adoption laws.

We asked him to let Madame Berger know that Lisa and Ricardo would be coming to visit in mid-July. We hired our previous translator from the mission trips to help Lisa and Ricardo find the orphanage. Another adoptive mom from Knoxville was also traveling with Lisa.

Before the date they had all planned to meet, the translator tried to contact Madame Berger by phone, but she did
not answer his calls. On the day they were going to visit
Delivrans Mwen, the translator was very sick and unable to
meet them, so Lisa and Ricardo spent at least three hours on
their own, looking for the orphanage. I was doing my best,
with Shawn's help, to give them directions over the phone.
There were very few street signs in Port-au-Prince. It was just
a maze of streets that crisscross each other, indefinitely. After
giving up, they vowed to try again the next day, in hope of
meeting up with the translator. The translator was still getting no answer from Madame Berger by phone.

The next day, the translator was feeling well enough to
meet them, and they arrived apparently unannounced at the
orphanage. At first, Madame Berger would not even let them
in, though she was very familiar with the translator and had
been told by Pastor Odson to be expecting Lisa and Ricardo.
After much discussion through the iron front door, she
finally conceded and at least let them into the front room.
Thankfully, Lisa is fluent in Haitian Creole and was able to
participate in the discussions. She explained they were there
to meet Marvin, and they would be helping with the adoption. She asked if they could meet Marvin.

With much reluctance, it took Madame Berger nearly
thirty minutes to present him. Lisa said he was lethargic and
did not look well. She also stated that they did not see or
hear any other children around. We assumed they were
underneath the building in the room where they eat their
meals. Lisa and Ricardo were very suspicious that some of
the children we had met on our previous visits were not
really staying at the orphanage at all.

Needless to say, this visit did not go well, and we were
worried about the future cooperation of the madame. When

asked, she would not provide Lisa and Ricardo with any information about Marvin and his family. They were seeking to know if his parents were still alive, if he had a birth certificate, if he had siblings, and what his true story was. Marvin would need to go to several appointments during this process, such as getting passport photos taken, medical appointments, embassy appointments, and more. We needed her full cooperation to move forward. Lisa called me early the next morning to share the details of their visit. I tried not to get discouraged at the madame's level of resistance. After my conversation with Lisa, I called our friend Shawn, who was our church's contact for the orphanage, and we spoke for a long time about what Lisa had observed. He vowed to help gain some cooperation through Pastor Odson, and we felt relieved to have an ally like Shawn on our side.

DISTRACTED DRIVING

A funny side note…we were returning to Tennessee the morning that I received the phone call from Lisa. I was trying to pack up a week's worth of stuff and carry on a serious conversation at the same time. After we were all loaded in our vehicle, including one of Brooke's good softball friends, we hit the road toward home. As we traveled through a remote part of Florida, I proceeded to call Shawn while I was driving. I was deep in conversation when the speed limit quickly dropped from 65 mph, to 55, then to 45 (this is why distracted driving is a very bad idea). As I came flying down a marsh bridge, I saw a police officer and the 45 mph speed limit sign at the same time. The reason this was funny was that, as a former transportation safety engineer, I rarely drive more than a few miles over the speed limit and had never been pulled over for speeding in my life! The girls and Mike were absolutely cracking up at me, and I was mortified. Mike was busy snapping photos of the police car behind us so he could have a record of my indiscretion.

When the officer asked me if I knew how fast I was going, I really did not know. He informed me I was traveling 67 mph in a 45 mph zone. I had set my cruise control at 67 when the speed limit was 65 mph. My reaction was a quick, "No way! I am so sorry!" I was truly repentant and very polite to the officer. He took my information and proceeded back to his police car, while Mike continued to laugh at my misfortune. He came back to our vehicle and told me he was going to let me off with a warning (thank you, Lord!), and he said I did three things right. First, I did not argue with him. Second, I had no prior record or points on my license. Third, I was polite. He then asked me to guess how much my ticket would have been. It would have been a whopping $275! Boy, was I thankful he was in a forgiving mood. My lesson for that day: do not drive distracted, watch out for speed traps in rural Florida, and *always* treat police officers with respect!

Thankfully, in just a couple of days, Kelsey and I would be participating in another church-sponsored Haiti mission trip leaving on July 18. We could not wait to see Marvin again and hopefully gain some much-needed information. Because we were hoping to take care of some official adoption business, we planned for Mike to join us in Haiti on Sunday, July 22. We would be attending court in Jacmel, Haiti, to officially start the adoption process on the Haitian side. The signing in court needed to happen before they officially changed the adoption law. However, before we signed in court, we needed to know if Marvin had living parents. If his parents were still living, we would need their permission to adopt and their relinquishment of parental rights.

Madame had previously told us that Marvin was abandoned in the market. What we gathered was that his manman (Haitian for "mom") sat him down in the market and walked away, leaving him there alone. We assumed it was her hope that someone would pick him up and take care of him. I had a horrible time processing that this precious little boy had been abandoned in a market, as a baby, to fend for himself. As it turned out, this story could not have been further from the truth, but that was all we knew at this point in the process. We were also told that the father was deceased. We wondered how they would know this bit of information if he had been abandoned in the market, so we had many questions that needed answering before we could proceed.

CHAPTER 6

Birth-Mom Search

*God also testified to it by signs, wonders and various
miracles, and by gifts of the Holy Spirit distributed
according to his will.*
—HEBREWS 2:4

In July 2012, our mission trip group arrived in Port-au-
Prince on a Thursday, ready to hit the ground running. As
usual, there was a swirl of activity upon arrival. I could not
wait to see Marvin again, as well as all the kids we had grown
to love in this short time.

The airline had misplaced seven pieces of our group's
luggage. It was going to be a long week if those pieces did not
show up soon. Thankfully, they did arrive later that day, and
a small group of us ran back to the airport to retrieve them.

We were able to visit Delivrans Mwen on our first day,
and it was wonderful to hold my future son in my arms
again. I wondered if he remembered me. It really seemed so,
but I was also sure he soaked up all the love and affection
any visitors brought his way. I later found out from a different mission group staying at the guest house that they all
knew and loved Marvin. I was not surprised, because there
was just something special about him.

Facebook Entry: July 19, 2012

When we got to the orphanage, Marvin was sound asleep in the middle of the floor! Of course I had to snuggle until he woke up. After he got his bearings, I got that awesome neck hug. Love him soooo much. Also, successfully retrieved all 7 pieces of luggage. Nothing short of a miracle, LOL!

When we arrived, I was sad to see him sleeping on the cold tile floor. With no adult to tell you when to take a nap, you just fall asleep wherever you are playing. I also realized he could have been lying there because it was cooler than the beds. I transferred him to a bottom bunk, and he settled back into sleep. After his nap was over, I picked him up and we walked around the orphanage's upper level. He spotted his friend Tyre out in the streets, and his face lit up as he shouted his name. Up until this point, we were not sure that Marvin could talk. This was a reassuring sound to our ears.

Shawn was on this trip as well and had agreed to help us in any way he could. He had known the madame and Pastor Odson a lot longer than we had, and they both trusted and respected Shawn. He would prove to be an invaluable ally in the whole process.

That first day at Delivrans Mwen, we set out right away to have some discussions with the madame about Marvin. We used the translator that the mission group used, Peterson, and she used her translator, a gentleman named Makenson. Makenson had given us an uneasy feeling, but she wanted him around, and she did not care for our translator. Most of the time she would not speak to him or even look him in the eyes. Madame was blaming Peterson for the whole situation when Lisa and Ricardo came to visit.

BIRTH CERTIFICATE SEARCH

Shawn discussed with Madame Berger the need for her cooperation with Ricardo whenever he required access to Marvin. He explained that we would use a secret code any time we would send someone to the orphanage to get Marvin, and that she was to provide the access if they used the secret code. We also asked her for details of Marvin's life. At this point, she revealed that Marvin's manman was alive, and that she had contacted her right after Lisa and Ricardo had visited. She told us that the birth mom was very interested in allowing us to adopt Marvin. Even as the story evolved and lies were revealed, that was a breath of fresh air for my soul.

We told the madame that Mike was flying in on Sunday and that we were heading to court to sign our initial intent to adopt. We stressed that it was very important that we meet Marvin's birth mom before we signed in court. Half of the Haitian lawyer's fee was due when we signed, and if his mother was not on board, it would be a waste of money to start the process. Madame said she hadn't heard from her since that day after Lisa's visit, but that she would try to get in touch with her. Madame also revealed that Marvin had a birth certificate on file at the orphanage. We asked to see it and take a picture of it. She was not very excited about producing the birth certificate, but we managed to take a quick picture of it.

In the excitement of the moment, I just snapped the picture and gave the document back to her. I did not look closely at the certificate that was written in French. Later that evening, as I was studying it, I realized she had shown us the birth certificate of another child instead. Now I was going to have to wait until the next day to see if she would show us Marvin's actual birth certificate. I could not help wondering whether this was an honest mistake or was done on purpose. Later that evening, Shawn and I had a meeting with Pastor Odson. We explained the importance of finding the birth mom before Monday.

At this time, we also explained that Marvin would have to move to Lisa's orphanage, Chante Lajwa, in Camatin about three hours away. After his birth mom went to court and relinquished her rights to us and Chante Lajwa, Marvin would be allowed to move to the orphanage assigned to his care. Because of the difficulty we were having with Madame Berger, we were hoping to move him on this trip. We knew this would be a long shot, and Pastor Odson was reluctant because we did not yet have the birth mom's permission. I understood his reservations, but he agreed he would do everything in his power to help find Marvin's mother.

The next day, when we returned to the orphanage in the afternoon, we again asked Madame Berger if we could see Marvin's birth certificate. She reluctantly went to a closet in the kitchen and returned with a name and a birthdate written on a piece of paper. This was not what we had asked for and she knew it. She reluctantly headed back to the kitchen and finally retrieved a second birth certificate. We wondered why she was so resistant to our every request. I looked closely this time and determined that it was indeed Marvin's birth certificate. At this point, we also realized that Marvin's name was actually Marvens. We had originally thought it was Mauvens, based on the way they were pronouncing it. As you may have guessed, when Marvin came home and we officially adopted him in Tennessee, we also changed his legal name to Marvin.

There was no father listed on his birth certificate, and the mother's name was listed as Roselina. We would later discover that his birth certificate was considered incomplete, but having an incomplete certificate was better than no birth certificate at all. The birth certificates in Haiti must be stamped and approved by several offices to be considered official. The certificate revealed that Marvin was born on August 8, 2010. According to this birth certificate, he was almost two years old.

CHURCH AND BEACH

We spent the rest of the day playing with the children and Marvin, of course. It was always good just to play a few simple games, get our hair braided by the older girls, and love on the children. Some favorite activities included bubbles, coloring, punching balloons, Play-Doh, and face painting. The group did an excellent job of being present for the kids and providing them a much-needed break from the monotony of orphanage living. I was grateful and thankful for everyone on this trip. I tried hard not to "take over" this mission trip with our needs for Marvin's adoption. Everyone

The "play" room in the orphanage

was super supportive in flexibility, and I know in prayer as well.

On Sunday, Mike was scheduled to arrive while the group would be away from Port-au-Prince. I had made prior arrangements for him to be picked up from the airport and taken to the guest house. I was slightly worried because once he arrived in Haiti, we would have no way of reaching each other to communicate any change of plans that could happen on either end.

The group attended church that morning with all the children from the orphanage. Kelsey hung out with Marvin, and I spent time with Sofiani. I knew I would be back again soon, but I was not sure how long it would be before Kelsey would see Marvin again. I wanted to make sure she got adequate sister/brother bonding time on this trip. I have a beau-

Marvin and Kelsey on the way to church

tiful photo of Kelsey holding Marvin in her lap on the bus, with Marvin smiling from ear to ear.

After we attended church, which in Haiti was on average two to three hours long, we planned to take all the children to a private beach we had secured. We went back to the guest house and changed the children into the swimming suits we had brought for them, fed them some lunch, and then loaded all of us onto the bus. We were so crowded, sitting three to four in a seat. It was a long, hot drive, but it would be worth it.

Marvin's first trip to the beach

Most of the children were initially fearful of the ocean, but warmed up to the water pretty quickly. Marvin, however, did not. He would not leave my arms or Kelsey's and did not even want to have the water touch his feet. We also found out he was petrified of dogs, when a young dog came snooping around our group. Most dogs in Haiti are not "family pets," but are usually wild and are competition for food. Not surprisingly, Marvin to this day is still petrified of dogs.

After the beach excursion, all forty-plus of us piled into the small bus for the hour-and-a-half ride back to the orphanage. It was quite a challenge getting everyone loaded onto the bus, and then…the bus would not start. After about fifteen minutes, we all piled off the bus and waited for the local men to make repairs to the bus. Thank the Lord, about an hour later they were able to get it running again, and we all reboarded the bus. That bus ride gave new meaning to the word *closeness*.

MIKE'S ARRIVAL

On the way back, I found out through Lisa that Mike's flight had been delayed. Because she knew how to reach the driver I had secured for Mike, I was communicating with her back in the States. They finally picked up Mike, but neither Jameson nor Mike could find the guest house. Lisa gave me a phone number to reach Jameson. I called his number and handed the phone to our translator to communicate with him for me. I asked our translator to give him directions to the guest house. He had a five-minute conversation and finally passed the phone to our bus driver to give him more directions. After the conversation ended, I looked closely at the phone and realized that I dialed the wrong number. I was shocked that they had both participated in this conversation, and the stranger on the other end never revealed that he had no idea what they were talking about! We laughed about that for a good long time. We finally reached Jameson and succeeded in having Mike dropped off at the guest house.

That evening, the other couple from our church who were interested in adopting had scheduled a meeting with a US adoption representative who happened to be in Port-au-Prince at the time. This couple, Mike, Shawn, and Pastor Odson all ventured out in the late afternoon to meet with this representative at a local hotel. After their meeting, they were planning on visiting the orphanage to see if they had located Marvin's birth mom and to learn her whereabouts. I chose not to go because I was not feeling well and knew Mike was better suited to handle some of the tough negotiations. This trip was a dangerous one because they would all be out in Port-au-Prince at night, which was never a safe choice. Thankfully, nothing happened.

They arrived safely at the orphanage and apparently had a heated discussion by lantern with the madame. Our church would later install electricity, but at this point the orphanage was without power. It was clear she was not cooperating nor making any effort to find his birth mom. Mike was trying very hard to stress the importance of this. We were about to miss our only window of opportunity to adopt Marvin if we did not find his birth mom. Pastor Odson vowed again to do everything he could to help.

When Mike arrived back at the guest house late that night, we had a long discussion and prayed about whether it was wise to go to court the next day. We had planned on going to court on Monday, and Mike was scheduled to fly back on Tuesday, while I was scheduled to fly back with the group on Wednesday. We made calls to the States to discuss with Lisa what we should do. They made it very clear that once Mike and I signed in court, half of the lawyer's fee would be due regardless of whether we found the birth mom or not. We prayed and sought God's guidance on whether we should move forward. Then we both fell asleep in our respective boys' or girls' bunk rooms, exhausted from a day of dead ends.

MORE NEGOTIATIONS

On Monday, Mike and I split off from the mission group and were picked up by Ricardo. The plan was for us to meet with Madame Berger together and see if we could persuade her to share any contact information for Marvin's birth mom. If we could find her, and she was willing, we would still go to court in Jacmel on Monday. The mission group, which included Kelsey, headed to the other orphanage in Carrefour. We told them that if we were able to find his birth mom, we would be heading to court in Jacmel that day and would not be at Delivrans Mwen when they arrived after lunch. If we did not find his birth mom, we would be waiting for them at the orphanage.

Unfortunately, the meeting with Madame Berger, Ricardo, Mike, and I did not go well. It was so difficult to just sit there as they went back and forth in Haitian Creole and to not understand a word they were saying. Haitians can be very harsh with each other, and this was obviously no exception. We were getting nowhere. Madame still claimed that no one had heard from Marvin's birth mom in days. Ricardo left the orphanage and agreed to give us until tomorrow morning to make a decision. Sadly, we were still at the orphanage when the mission group returned from their visit in Carrefour. We had big decisions to make in less than twenty-four hours. If we were to go forward, Jameson would pick us up at 7:00 a.m. on Tuesday to head over the mountain to court in Jacmel.

CHAPTER 7

Our Day in Haitian Court

But let all who take refuge in you be glad; let them ever sing for joy. Spread your protection over them, that those who love your name may rejoice in you.
—PSALM 5:11

Taking a leap of faith, still with no contact with Marvin's birth mom, we were picked up bright and early on Tuesday morning and headed to the lawyer's home to pick him up. Our court appearance would happen in Jacmel, which was at least three hours away from Port-au-Prince without traffic. We had a tight schedule to keep, and traffic in and out of Port-au-Prince could be brutal. I knew we needed everything to go exactly as planned or we would miss our day in court.

Upon arrival at the lawyer's home, we sat outside for twenty grueling minutes before he finally arrived in his three-piece suit ready for court. He had accidentally over-slept. Jameson spoke limited English, and the lawyer spoke even less, so we headed on our journey in relative silence. Navigating the traffic of Port-au-Prince, we finally reached the mountains and were in for the ride of our life. I liken it to driving through the Smoky Mountains at 60 miles per hour, honking the horn as you go around the blind corners just in case someone was in your lane, which happened a lot. I was a nervous wreck and tried to focus on the beautiful scenery of the mountainous region.

At the same time as our Tuesday journey began, Shawn and Pastor Odson began their own journey to find Marvin's birth mom. They were going to take this search into their own hands. Overnight, Pastor Odson had received a few tips on where she might be living, who was related to her, and a possible phone number for a relative. They drove around a few areas of Port-au-Prince and inquired of her whereabouts, then they stopped by Pastor Odson's church. While they were outside of his church, they met up with a parishioner named Jerome. He spoke very good English. I think he was bored, because he asked if he could go along with them that day. The three of them headed back out with a possible phone number for a relative of Marvin's.

When they called the number, her brother answered and said he was not sure where she was. I believe he mentioned she had been visiting family. He was able to provide a possible phone number for her, and the first thing Shawn did was "top up" her cell phone. In Haiti, that means to add minutes to her cell phone using a mobile app named Digicell. To my knowledge, all cell phones in Haiti are on a pay-as-you-go plan where you pay for minutes upfront. Shawn assumed correctly that no one had been able to reach her because she did not have any minutes left on her phone. After the top off, he called, and she answered immediately.

Pastor Odson explained why they were trying to reach her, and she agreed to let them pick her up and bring her back to the mission house. After days of getting nowhere, they had finally found the needle in the haystack! Mike and I had no idea as we were traveling through the mountains trusting God that we were going to find the birth mom.

OVER THE MOUNTAIN

On the other side of the mountain, we turned off the paved road onto a dirt road. We recognized the sizeable home at the end of the dirt road as Chante Lajwa, the orphanage that Ricardo ran. We were told by Jameson that they needed to stop here briefly. I asked to use the restroom and when I was finished a lady introduced herself as Ricardo's mother. We had heard her name and knew that she and her husband had started the orphanage many years before. She proceeded to tell Mike and me that the madame at Delivrans Mwen was lying to us, and that we were never going to find the birth mom. She told us we should not go to court to sign. She also mentioned that she had several boys for adoption and showed us their pictures. We felt like the breath had been sucked right out of us. We did not want to adopt just any boy, we wanted to adopt our son, the child we were sure God had placed in our lives for that very reason. We politely declined, and she asked us to sit in her office.

While there, the lawyer dropped a bombshell on us, stating that we could not go to court after all. We were flabbergasted and had many questions swirling around our minds. What was happening? Why had we come all the way here? What had been miscommunicated that now we were not going to be able to sign in court? It seemed like the world was falling apart, and it was happening fast. I felt physically sick to my stomach.

The lawyer stepped away from us, and we could tell he was having a phone conversation with Pastor Odson. We had no idea what they were talking about, and we were trying really hard not to panic. Maybe I should reword that. I was trying hard not to panic; typically, Mike does not panic about anything. We were certain God was not closing this door. I texted Lisa in the States and asked her if she knew what was going on. Thankfully, she was able to immediately call me on Jameson's phone and told me not to panic, that she also was trying to figure out what was going on. The lawyer hung up with Pastor Odson and continued a conversation with Ricardo's mother. After several discussions back and forth, the lawyer announced, "Okay, we go to court!" We never found out what the problem was while we were waiting at the orphanage, or why suddenly everything was good to go. We had resolved to ourselves that, during this process, sometimes it would just be that way—sometimes the language barrier was unsurmountable, and we just had to accept that and move forward.

We quickly piled back in the car and headed down the other side of the mountain toward Jacmel, but we barely made it out of the driveway before we turned around again. Mike and I were asking ourselves, "Now what?" It turned out that they had forgotten to pick up a set of birthparents who were coming with us to court. They were heading to court to relinquish their parental rights so that their child could also be adopted and placed in a forever home in the States. Their faces looked sad, but friendly. They had a grown son with them. The mom climbed into the back seat of the small Honda CR-V and the very tall dad and son climbed into the back of the hatchback. Mike and I felt terrible that they had to ride back there, but they were adamant that we stay put.

My guess was they could not afford another child, and probably had several other children at home. This, in fact, turned out to be the sad situation. It is the harsh reality for so many families in Haiti. I read somewhere that eighty-five percent of the population was unemployed. There just are not even close to enough jobs for a huge portion of the country.

Once we hit the road again, we received a phone call from Shawn. He called to tell us that he had found Marvin's birth mom, Roselina, and that they had picked her up and were headed to the guest house! He told me she was really looking forward to meeting us and was willing to wait all day for us to return. We hung up the phone, and I raised my arms in praise to our Lord. Only He could have made this possible! We rode the remaining twenty minutes to town in complete awe of His goodness.

COURT IN JACMEL

When we arrived in Jacmel, Jameson dropped the lawyer off at the court building. It reminded me of something out of a movie. It was a white, two-story building with huge wooden shutters flanking the windows and doors, which were propped open to provide some relief from the heat. We were not sure what to expect, but that was not it. Jacmel was very crowded, as were most of Haitian cities. We pulled away and found a side street to park on while we waited for the lawyer. After about a half hour, Jameson said it was time, and he drove us back to the court building.

We entered and went to a back office that had a few desks in it. We were directed to sit at the far desk. The clerk asked for our passports and proceeded to show us a spiral-bound notebook where the letter "X" and a line had been drawn for our signatures. We were instructed to print our names below our signatures, and they wrote our passport number under our names. That was it; that was the signing in court! We thanked them profusely and headed out to the car. Again, that was not at all what we expected, but we were learning to go with the flow.

AUTOMATIC WEAPONS

When we were finished at court, all seven of us loaded into the CR-V and headed back up the mountain. We dropped the other family off before we reached the orphanage. The July heat was close to one hundred degrees that day. We had been sweating profusely ever since we landed in Haiti. Mike decided that he could not stand it any longer and took his shirt off while we were in the backseat. On the way back, we passed a security checkpoint with machine-gun-armed guards. We were not sure why they decide to stop a vehicle, but Jameson told us they are mostly checking for proper vehicle registration.

As we passed through the checkpoint, two armed soldiers motioned for Jameson to pull over. They proceeded to approach the car and have a stern conversation with Jameson. They kept looking back at us, and Mike and I were smiling and waving as friendly as possible. I was trying not to stress; I really did not want to spend time in a Haitian jail for any perceived offense. After conversing with both Jameson and the lawyer, they finally let us continue on our journey.

As we pulled away, we asked them what that was all about, and they started to laugh. They said the guards wanted to know why Mike was not wearing a shirt. They told the guards that Mike was feeling sick, while Mike was not exactly corroborating this story by smiling and waving at them from the backseat. Needless to say, I punched Mike in the arm and told him to put his shirt on, "Now!" Apparently in Haiti, you are not allowed to ride in cars without wearing your shirt. Who knew? After a very long, but successful, day we reached Port-au-Prince just in time for afternoon rush hour.

MEETING ROSELINA

When we finally arrived at the mission house, Roselina was waiting for us on the upper porch. Shawn had done an excellent job of entertaining her all afternoon. She had lunch, looked at photos of our family from Facebook, taken a nap, and shared some details of her life with Shawn and Jerome. They had the guest house to themselves, because the mission group had left that morning to do their decompression day at a nearby beach resort. We had sent Kelsey on with the group, so she still had no idea that we had found Roselina. We could not wait to get in touch with her to share the good news, but communication with them was not working.

Upon our arrival, we spent several hours getting to know Roselina and helped her to know more about us. We were surprised at how young she looked. She was twenty-three years old. She was slender, tall, and had beautiful eyelashes, just like Marvin. According to his mom, he was about five months old when the earthquake happened. On that fateful day in January, Roselina told us that she had heard a loud noise and thought a vehicle had crashed into the small cinder-block home where she was staying. She ran outside to see what had happened, not realizing it was the earthquake that had made the loud crashing sound. After she exited, the full force of the quake struck, and the house fell down around Marvin. We were sure she was absolutely panicked.

When they were able to dig Marvin out of the rubble, they found that the cinder block had fallen all around him but not on him. She found her precious son, surrounded by cinder blocks and completely unharmed. As she was telling us this story, I was almost sobbing. We knew right then and there, God had big plans for our son. He spared his life for a purpose, and we felt privileged to see, firsthand, that purpose fulfilled. She said that people were calling him "little god" after the quake.

She also shared that she had two other children, his half-brother and half-sister, who were older than Marvin. She said the boy was six and the girl was four, but they were located in a different orphanage. She was sad because they were eating only once a day and were being mistreated there. She said she was hoping to move them to Delivrans Mwen if Madame Berger would take them in. Thankfully, we were able to transfer his Haitian brother and sister to Delivrans Mwen shortly after this visit. It was comforting to know Marvin would have siblings living with him for a short time. Sadly, with the laws about to change, we were too far along in the process to even consider adopting all three siblings.

Roselina shared that she had cared for Marvin for the first full year of his life. We did not realize at the time how crucial this would be to his stable child development. Bonding with a mother in those first few months is absolutely critical to a child's development. We would be forever grateful for the time they had together as mother and child.

She also told us that she was one of nine children in her family. She had already lost two siblings. As we were learning more about her, and vice versa, Pastor Odson returned to the guest house. He asked her if she had ever given her life to Christ. We will never forget this moment. Pastor Odson shared the gospel with her, then we all gathered in a circle and put our hands on Roselina as he led her to Christ. I was an emotional mess. We were so grateful that she was willing to entrust her son to us and was willing to let him go, because she knew it would mean a better life for him. We will never understand the heartbreak and pain she must have endured at this loss. But even more, we were overjoyed for her that she had trusted in Christ and found eternal life! We exchanged contact information and explained that Ricardo would be in touch with her soon regarding her court date and other requirements for the adoption.

Facebook Entry: July 24, 2012

Wow! All I can say is PRAISE JESUS!!! Today has been the most amazing test of faith & day of miracles. We pushed Mike's flight back to tomorrow with the plan of signing in court in Haiti to start the adoption process, which was a huge leap because there was a very good chance we would never find Marvin's mom. After looking for his mom for almost 2 weeks (6 days in person), we had just about given up last night. But…God whispered in our hearts to not give up.

We headed to Jacmel to court (3 hours over the mountain) & our dear friend went on a birth mom hunt this morning. This was after we had been told the mom hadn't been heard from by her family in 3 days. Only by God's miracle did they find her AND we got to meet her when we got back from court. AND…she accepted Christ under Pastor Odson's guidance. I WAS HOLDING HER HAND AS SHE ACCEPTED OUR SAVIOR!!! ABSOLUTELY AMAZING DAY. So many things happened & so many people to thank. It will be hard to leave tomorrow, but our spirits are lifted!

P.S. Marvin is somewhat of a miracle baby narrowly surviving the earthquake with rubble all around. I think God has big plans for my little man.

GOODBYES AND HELLOS

After sharing a meal together and sending Roselina on her way, we finally reached Kelsey and the group by telephone to share the good news. We updated the team that we would meet them at the airport for the return trip home. God was so good. As I lay in a hot Haitian bed that night, unable to sleep from the excitement of the day, there was only one way to describe what happened today, and that was that God came through big time.

The next morning, we made a quick trip to the orphanage to say goodbye one last time. It was hard to leave Marvin on the previous trip, but this time it was on a whole different level. He was going to be our son, Lord willing, and we were having to leave him behind with not enough food, love, or basic necessities. Marvin did not want us to leave and started crying. Even as young as he was, I think he knew there was a special bond between us. I cried my eyes out as we drove away and vowed to return as soon as possible.

We met back up with the team at the airport. It was awesome to hug Kelsey and share the excitement of the previous day with her in person. Even though she was eighteen, it was a relief to be reunited with her again. Haiti was an amazing place, but also a dangerous one, and we were glad the whole group made it safely back to the airport. It was a glorious reunion, as all the people on the mission trip had been praying and walking through this action-packed part of the journey with us. Everyone was overwhelmed, and probably a little bit surprised, that we were moving forward in the process.

No trip to Haiti was complete without an adventure of some sort. When we were waiting to go through security, Shawn realized that he forgot to put his satchel of tools in his checked baggage. He always traveled with them in case repairs were needed at either orphanage. Since he had no room in his carry-on bag, he asked Mike if he had any extra room in his carry-on. Mike agreed, and we all proceeded through security. As you can imagine, the security people did not like the fact that Mike had all sorts of tools in his bag. They made him go back to the check-in counter and check his carry-on bag. As they ushered him away, he disappeared around the corner, but I could not go back. I was hoping he would make it back through in time. I was worried we were going to have to leave him behind with no way of communicating with him. This day and age, we really take for granted our cell phones and the instant communication ability they provide.

Thankfully, Mike made it back through security with just enough time to board the plane. At that point, the group had already nicknamed him "Just Mike." On this and previous trips, we would be loaded up as a group and counting heads to make sure everyone was on board, and they would surmise that the only person missing was "Just Mike." Remember, I shared that we have the reverse of typical married roles. For all the years of our married life, I have been the one waiting on my husband so that we could leave the house. Even when the girls were teenagers, the three women would be waiting in the car on Sunday morning for Mike to finally arrive so we could go to church! Mike just is not in a hurry to arrive anywhere. However, I am grateful he hurried back through security so he wouldn't miss this flight. I'm pretty sure the pilot would not wait for him!

CHAPTER 8

Missed Court Date

*"Look at the birds of the air; they do not sow or reap
or store away in barns, and yet your heavenly Father
feeds them. Are you not much more valuable than
they? Can any one of you by worrying add a single
hour to your life?"*
—MATTHEW 6:26,27

After we arrived home, life returned to our new normal. We began preparing Kelsey for her freshman year of college at Samford University, in Birmingham, Alabama, and preparing Brooke for her freshman year of high school. Things sure were quiet around the house when Kelsey left for school. I am sure Brooke was thrilled to be the only target of parental conversation.

Lisa and Ricardo began working to secure a court date for Roselina to go to Jacmel and sign over her parental rights, giving the new orphanage, Chante Lajwa, permission to care for Marvin in the wake of that termination. A court date was set for September 4, another month away. On that day, I received a call from Lisa that Roselina did not show up. I did not have international calling on my cell phone, so I ran to Walgreens to purchase a calling card. In the Walgreens parking lot, I called Pastor Odson and received no answer. I then called Shawn and begged for his help. I texted Ricardo to try to find out what was going on. We were just devastated that she did not show up, but we found out later that she was uncomfortable because she did not know Jameson and was concerned about riding in a car with a stranger for hours.

During this delay, we wondered how we would cope if something happened to her, or she changed her mind. At this point, we were far into the process and were very emotionally connected to our son. We did not want to consider the possibility of not being able to bring him home. I think every adoptive parent can relate to this feeling. You hate to entertain those thoughts, but they are ever looming in the back of your mind. You hold your breath and guard a little piece of your heart, until the final steps of your adoption are complete and your child is legally yours forever.

On September 6, we received word that the court had called to reschedule for September 10. Major prayers were going on by us as well as our family and friends. At 9:46 a.m. on the morning of the tenth, I received news that Roselina had been successfully picked up by Jameson and they were on their way to Jacmel. Lisa had spoken to her recently and helped alleviate her fears of traveling with Jameson. I was so overwhelmed with emotion; I fell on my knees next to my bed and wept in thanks to the Lord.

Facebook Entry: September 10, 2012

She signed & they are on their way back to Port-au-Prince. Thank you, LORD! Beyond humble & grateful… Now only about 20 steps have to happen in Haiti, but this was a giant leap!!!

The fall continued in busy fashion, as usual. Brooke and I made plans to attend the next church mission trip to Haiti, which would take place in mid-October. I was so ready to see our son again. It would be almost three months since we had last seen him. I often wondered if he stopped waiting for our return, or if he was too young to understand at all. The latter was probably the case, and maybe that would be easier on his little heart anyway. I just prayed that his heart would be protected during this long, arduous process, and maybe a little prayer for our hearts, too. We were preparing to move Marvin to Lisa's orphanage in the near future, but were unprepared for the obstacles ahead and how long the process would take.

We arrived in Haiti, on October 18, 2012. There was a feeling of excitement by the whole group, as some were returning members and others were on their first trip. When we made it to the orphanage, the large steel door was opened for us, and there was a mass of children packed in the first room, so excited we had come. I quickly scanned the crowd to look for my boy, and there he was, several children back. I tried to weave my way through the sweet, familiar faces, to get to our son. His eyes lit up when he saw my face. My heart skipped a beat. I felt the Lord saying, "See, he does remember you. Don't worry, I have this under control."

Facebook Entry: October 18, 2012

Got to hold my baby again! I got my big neck hug, love him so much. He's not been feeling well, but he perked up at the end of our visit. I'm too exhausted to think straight, but will post more tomorrow...

The second day in Haiti, our group went to a local school supply store. It was very clean and well organized. With Pastor Odson's help, we had gathered a list of the necessary textbooks for every child in the orphanage. With probably twenty-five school-aged children, this was quite a task. Up to this point, the children had been homeschooled by the madame of the orphanage, but with our help, they were now attending Pastor Odson's school in Port-au-Prince. This was an amazing opportunity for them. This day was busy and full of things to accomplish, but I was disappointed I did not get to see Marvin since he was in school during the day. The children attend school as early as three years old in Haiti, where education is highly valued. Having to wait one more day to see our son again, I settled into a fitful sleep in my bunk at the guest house.

The following day, we played with and loved on the children of Delivrans Mwen in the morning and then headed to the Foyer des Amis orphanage in Carrefour in the afternoon. Marvin came with us to Carrefour, and he seemed to be a little overwhelmed at the other orphanage. They played loud

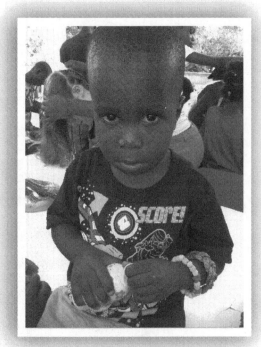

Marvin at the other orphanage,
looking unsure

music, and there are much older children at Foyer des Amis. I was pretty sure Marvin did not know what to make of it all. I took a precious picture of him with the most pitiful little pout on his face. He made one thing clear: he was not going to let go of me or Brooke under any circumstance, so we were more than happy to hold him the entire time.

After finishing our visit in Carrefour, we all loaded up in the school bus for the often long, traffic-laden trip back to the guest house in Port-au-Prince. Halfway there, Marvin told our translator, Peterson, that he had to go to the bathroom, and it was not number one. Oh boy, I thought, what in the world are we going to do? It was not like you could pull over at a gas station or rest stop to use the restroom. Haiti does not have public restrooms, and certainly not along the road, like we do in the States. Peterson had an idea. We would pull over to the side of the road and let Marvin use one of the holes in the sidewalk. I wondered what those holes were for, and now I knew, but I could not imagine him using it.

The bus pulled over and Peterson took Marvin out onto the sidewalk. Poor Marvin, he was terrified and was having none of it! He would not go and returned to the bus. I was proud of him—he made it all the way back to the guest house without using the bathroom. He might have been young, but he was determined. We were excited that Marvin would be able to spend the night with us at the guest house. He ate a huge dinner, polishing off an enormous plate of delicious Haitian food. This was probably the most diverse meal he had ever eaten, and I hoped it would not cause stomach problems later in the evening. Thankfully, it did not.

We got Marvin showered and ready for bed. This was my first opportunity to really take on the role of "mom," and I relished every moment of it. The kids in the orphanage wash every day with a bucket of cold water dumped over their head, after lathering up with soap. I knew Marvin would not have any trouble with the cold guest house shower. It was still shocking to get in that cold water, but he did great. After cleaning up, we prayed and tucked him in to a bottom bunk. As he fell fast asleep, I just thanked God for this precious child, and prayed that he would be in his own bed in Knoxville, sooner rather than later. Little did I know, it would be nineteen more months before he could be under our roof, tucked safely into bed.

Later that evening, I woke to a thump and a cry. Marvin had fallen out of the bottom bed and onto the floor. Thankfully, he was not hurt, just a little shaken up. I did not realize that he might have problems sleeping in the bed, forgetting that multiple children always shared a mattress at the orphanage, and being young, he was probably always on the inside. We cradled some pillows and items around him to keep him from falling out again, and he fell fast asleep for the rest of the night.

Facebook Entry: October 20, 2012

Spent the entire day with Marvin and are enjoying a sleepover with him at the guest house. What a day, lots of bonding!! Monday will be hard.

On Monday, October 22, we had to leave Haiti behind. Brooke and I had enjoyed every minute of bonding with Marvin. We, of course, had other children that stole our hearts from both orphanages. It is hard to describe the heartache you feel being the recipient of the deep longing to be loved from an orphan child. It was overwhelming at times.

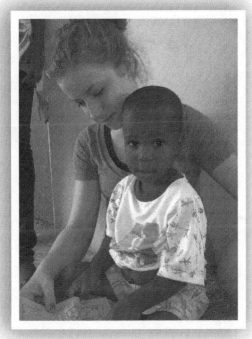

Brooke and Marvin bonding together

We took Marvin back to the orphanage and helped the workers get the children dressed for school. It was a mishmash of socks, school uniforms, appropriate school shoes, and matching hair ribbons. I could not imagine getting that many children ready for school each morning, and I had a new appreciation for Madame Berger and her few workers. As we were standing with the children in the front room, waiting for their ride to school, Marvin kept desperately saying something to me, over and over again. He had these sad little eyes, pleading with me to understand what he was saying. He kept saying, "Grangou, grangou," and wanted me to pick him up. I could not remember the meaning of the word, so I asked Peterson to help. Peterson shared with me that "grangou" meant "hungry." This just tore at the inner depths of this mother's heart. I knew he was often hungry, but to hear him say he was hungry directly to me, and pleading to me for help, was almost too much to bear. We had fed him breakfast, but he was still hungry. I could not feed him snacks in front of the other children, but how could I leave my baby hungry? I quickly snuck him a few goldfish and hugged him tight. I hoped he knew how much I loved him and wanted to bring him home, right then and there.

After their transportation arrived, it was time to say goodbye. The school was too far, and the route was too dangerous to walk, so our church was providing a "Tap Tap" to take the children to school. "Tap Tap" literally means "quick quick," and I can assure you they all drive quick! A "Tap Tap" in Haiti was a small pickup truck, outfitted with a cover and benches in the bed of the truck. They are brightly decorated with painted designs. When a passenger wants to get off, they

Ready for school

"tap" the roof of the cover to let the driver know. The children all piled into the back of this "Tap Tap," and almost immediately some of the older girls started to sob hysterically. Marvin and the younger children would be having school at the orphanage that day, so we brought him back into the front foyer area. As I struggled with tears, our sweet son rubbed my back while I held him on my hip. He also offered an uninitiated kiss. Melt my heart!! Brooke and I loved on Marvin as long as possible and then began the difficult task of leaving. He really started to cry as we made our way to the bus. In my heart, I was asking, "Why do I have to leave him, Lord?"

I knew this was a long process, but it really, really hurt. We were all an emotional wreck as the "Tap Tap" pulled away carrying the sounds of deep sadness with it, and the door to the orphanage was closed and locked. We all boarded our bus and rode along in a strange quiet, as we silently cried it out and then tried to compose ourselves. This was one of the hardest things I have ever had to do. It was just getting harder and harder to leave.

Facebook Entry: October 22, 2012

Landed safely in Miami, soooo hard to leave today, praying we can bring our son home soon. Today he kissed me & rubbed my back when I was holding him. He also told me he was hungry & to pick him up & feed him. I will continually leave a piece of my heart in Haiti. I'm also madly in love with the girl, Sofiani, in this pix. I wept as the older kids left in their Tap Tap for their new school as they were weeping too. Then wept again as I said goodbye to Marvin (he bawled too). Such a hard day, but so thankful to be able to go. Thank you Lord!

*The children crying as they leave for school
in the Tap Tap*

In November 2012, we had to do a home study amendment, because Kelsey was now eighteen years old, and they had forgotten to ask the questions of Kelsey separately. Usually, the parents can answer questions for the children. USCIS also required more information from Kelsey, as they had accidentally inserted my name instead of hers on some of the paperwork. These were just two more hurdles to jump through in our long journey. Of course, this new home study amendment had to be translated, certified, authenticated, and sent to the Haitian Consulate, as well. On the Haitian side of things, the Haitian lawyer would have to match this up with our dossier that was already in Haiti. Thankfully, a mission team was going to visit Chante Lajwa in December, and they were willing to hand deliver it for us.

CHAPTER 9

Embassy and Bonding Trip

*"I have told you this so that my joy may be in
you and that your joy may be complete."*
—JOHN 15:11

It was New Year's Day 2013, and I had spent the last couple
of days visiting with my extended family in Georgia. My
dad, Charlie, and my stepmom, Lucy, joined us for our
annual Christmas celebration. My brother, Steve, his wife,
Amy, and my two nephews, Jack and Nick, were gracious
hosts, as usual.

I spent quite a bit of my time finalizing my plans to visit
Haiti by myself. I had said I would never go by myself, yet
here I was preparing to leave the next day. Unfortunately, I
can be somewhat stubborn when I set my mind on something. The original plan was for Lisa and me to travel
together. However, airfare to Port-au-Prince over the holidays was outrageous. Lisa had to go for work with her non-
profit, but I just could not justify the extra expense. When I
had almost given up on being able to go at all, I stumbled
upon a lower priced airline that flies to Port-au-Prince. The

only catch was I would have to actually spend the night in Fort Lauderdale, Florida, but I thought it would be worth it. As I was leading up to my day of departure, I ran around Suwanee, Georgia, getting ready for my trip. Passport? Check. Cash? Check. Clothing and gifts for Marvin? Check. Snacks for both of us? Check. Emergency medicine? Check. Emergency contact information? Check. Gifts for hosts? Check.

I am the ultimate planner and list maker, so I spent a lot of time reorganizing my belongings. Plus, this new airline allowed only forty pounds for a checked bag, and that was very hard to do when traveling to a third-world country. Mid-morning, I checked my flight status to find it had been delayed several hours. I had passed on an earlier ride to the airport with my Dad and Lucy, as Amy offered to take me later. As my six o'clock flight was delayed to after nine o'clock, I began to regret the upcoming overnight stay in Fort Lauderdale.

Amy dropped me at the airport and my flight finally left, several hours delayed. When I finally arrived in Fort Lauderdale and took the shuttle to my hotel, it was 12:30 a.m. I was also very surprised when I realized the "hotel" I chose was really a motel with doors to the outside. Of course, my room was the very last one, as far away from the lobby as you could get. I sped-walked and prayed all the way down the walkway until I reached my room, slammed the door shut, and locked it. What was I thinking, and how could I have missed that detail when I booked my room? This would be one of the many lessons to be learned when traveling to and from Haiti.

BACK TO HAITI AGAIN

I got only about two and a half hours of sleep before I had to catch the 5:00 a.m. shuttle back to the airport. For some reason, I could not sleep (sarcasm alert). Of course, when I arrived at the airport, I discovered that my next flight was already delayed a couple of hours. I sure hoped this would not be a consistent pattern with this airline. I regretted my cost savings already. As you can imagine, it was a little difficult to communicate with people in Haiti that my flight was two hours delayed. When I placed calls to Haiti, I would often get a recorded message in French. Probably something along the line of "All circuits are busy, please try again later."

When I finally made it to Port-au-Prince, I discovered the newly renovated section of the airport was now open. I had heard that it was much better, and was it ever a huge improvement. It was very similar to other international/smaller country airports I had visited before. When I arrived in baggage claim, I was pleasantly surprised that only a few baggage handlers were present and they respected my refusal of help. Upon exiting the airport, I waited a short time before connecting with Pastor Odson. Anxious to see my son, we headed straight to Delivrans Mwen.

When we arrived, a few children greeted us and let us in the locked front door. It was always good to see their smiling faces and receive their welcoming hugs. These children lived for visitors. Of course, I was on a mission to immediately see my precious son. The children guided me down the stairs to the outside back section of the orphanage. I saw that most of the children were getting their bucket "shower" outside. As I searched the group for Marvin, he spotted me and smiled the biggest smile. His smile spoke to my heart, "You came to see me again!" He obediently stayed in line for his bath, while I helped dry off several of the kids and waited patiently for Marvin to finish his turn. Once done, I got his awesome neck hug. Boy, had I missed him. Pastor Odson left to make some hospital visits. Sadly, some of the children had contracted cholera and were very ill. Marvin and I headed upstairs where the kids were slowly finding clean clothes to wear. I noted how there was really no gender here when it came to clothes. If an item fit and they could get it on themselves, it was theirs for the day.

Many of the children who had been sick during our last visit in the fall now appeared much better. A tiny boy named Richardson and his twin sister, Richeline, look markedly improved. These children were around six years old but were the size of a typical two-year-old in America. Richeline barely weighed twenty pounds back in the fall. She looked strong and healthy and was finally getting a little meat on her bones and a little fire in her spirit. In December when another small group was visiting the orphanage, Richardson was having extreme swelling of his lower extremities, but this time I did not see any signs of swelling. Praise God! I got a quick, but excited hug from Sofiani, but I did not see her or her sister, Jacqueline, for the rest of my visit.

After I played with the kids for a while, Madame Berger said she wanted to speak to me through her translator, Makenson. I was quite nervous as I was alone and had no one else to communicate for me. I wondered if Makenson would even truthfully translate, but knew I just had to go with the flow for now. We sat down in the front room as the madame proceeded to tell me that she worked very, very hard, that she had no other job possibility, and that because of the orphanage she could not spend time with her family. She said she had invested some of her own money to keep the orphanage going.

Then she dropped the bomb on me, and flat out asked me to pay her for adopting Marvin. I was taken aback but composed myself enough to say that I was not allowed to pay her, because it was immoral and illegal. We ended the conversation, but I could tell my answer did not satisfy her in the least. I began to have some serious doubts about being able to get Marvin moved to Chante Lajwa without a fight. Marvin's manman had already signed in court, giving us permission to adopt and Chante Lajwa permission to care for him until the adoption was completed. Madame Berger had no legal right to keep Marvin with her, but I knew it would still be difficult to move him out of her orphanage. For this visit, I wanted to just focus on spending time with my future son.

MOTHER/SON BONDING

Pastor Odson arrived back at the orphanage, and I gathered up Marvin to head to our hotel, "Habitation Hatt." It is hard to compare the room to an American hotel, but for Haiti the accommodations were adequate, although quite expensive. In addition to the nightly rate, the biggest expense was the food at the hotel restaurant. I had chosen a hotel with a pool so that Marvin and I would have an activity to engage in while we were there. With the high cost of food, I was second-guessing my decision to stay in a hotel instead of the guest house.

Marvin and I ate dinner at the hotel restaurant, where he promptly ate half of a giant hamburger and all of his French fries. To this day, Marvin still loves hamburgers. He would have eaten the whole burger but I knew that would not be a good idea. Though I could tell he was very hungry, he had to take it slow. I must say that during all my visits, I absolutely loved most Haitian food. There is something I love about the spices and the slow cooking of the meat. The spiciness of some of the dishes, with the Caribbean flare, was right up my food palate alley. I was very grateful that I crossed paths with several excellent cooks.

Marvin's first restaurant meal
(funny, he doesn't like fries now)

I got Marvin showered again (because after a day of play with thirty-four of your friends, you are dirty again). When it was time for bed, he just lay down and stayed exactly where I put him in the bed. I guess this was one perk of adopting a child from an orphanage setting; they tend to be very obedient and not mess around when it comes to routines. Soon he was fast asleep, and I marveled at how precious he looked while sleeping. I missed him so much and prayed to the Lord that he would be coming home soon.

The next day, Pastor Odson picked us up and we headed to the Mega Mart. We bought some supplies for the orphanage such as rice, diapers, juice, snacks, and toiletries. After we unloaded all the supplies, Pastor Odson left me for a couple of hours at the orphanage by myself. I spent another fun afternoon hanging out with all the kids. Entertaining almost three dozen kids by myself, with my limited Haitian Creole, was definitely a challenge. We managed to make funny photos with the photo booth app on my iPad and went through the alphabet together on my virtual chalkboard. The rest of the time, we danced to music on my phone, played London Bridge, and the swing-me-upside-down game (basically, I held them up on my hip and then swung them upside down). I may have been getting a little too old to play that game and paid for it the next day with a sore back.

Just as they were serving lunch and Madame Berger was asking me if I wanted a plate, Pastor Odson showed up, and we headed out for the day. I narrowly escaped having to eat at the orphanage. I was sure the food was very tasty, but it was really not safe for me to eat. The last time some electricians from our church ate at the orphanage, several of them became very ill. I had a toddler to care for and could not afford to be suffering from Montezuma's Revenge! We picked up Roselina so she could spend time with us. I had brought some crafting supplies to teach Roselina how to make paper bead necklaces from magazines. My hope was she would learn to make these necklaces and be able to sell them for a little bit of income. We had some laughs as my paper kept tearing, but she caught on quick, and I left her with all the supplies I had brought. After Roselina left, Marvin and I spent until late afternoon at the hotel, playing. I tried to entice him into going in the pool again, but with no luck. It didn't help that the entire pool was about six feet deep, and I could not stand up in the water to show him it was safe. He would have none of the pool. The whole reason I wanted to stay at this hotel and not the guest house was so he would have the pool to swim in during the day. Oh well, at least the food was good and the accommodations were clean.

GETTING TO KNOW PASTOR ODSON

Later that evening, Pastor Odson and his wife joined us for dinner at the hotel. It was nice to finally meet his wife, as she lived in Miami with their children. During dinner, Pastor Odson shared a story with me that had happened about six years earlier. His youngest daughter, who was about twelve at the time, was kidnapped for ransom from their church. It was heartbreaking to hear this story, and I of course immediately assumed that it ended tragically. But it did not! The kidnappers contacted Pastor Odson and demanded fifty thousand dollars for her safe return. Being a pastor who has a clinic, an orphanage, several churches, and a school, they just assumed he could get his hands on that kind of money. He tried to explain that he could not raise that much money, but his pleas were falling on deaf ears. Word spread through the community, and many people gathered together to pray for her safe return. The kidnappers had taken her to a remote village area in the mountains. When those villagers noticed an unfamiliar girl at this house, they immediately contacted the authorities and then took matters into their own hands. They managed to attack the kidnappers and safely rescued his daughter. Some of the criminals escaped, but several were caught, and justice was served. I think Pastor Odson said his wife and all their children flew to Miami two days later and have lived there ever since.

I was just floored, and so grateful that God spared his daughter who was now attending college in the States. I had a true appreciation for the sacrifice he had made to serve the Lord in his country. He was separated from his family for months and years at a time, but he continued to press on. After a delightful outdoor meal, we said our goodbyes and planned to meet up again on Friday.

Facebook Entry: January 5, 2013:
Five things I learned about my son on this trip:1) he loves ketchup 2) he loves French fries (don't all kids?) 3) he does NOT like pancakes, raisins, or almonds 4) the most noise he ever makes is when he sleeps (maybe when he comes home for good, we can help slay those monsters of his dreams) 5) he is the best son ever!!! But I may be partial :-) Praying he comes home this summer. His mom has her embassy appointment at the end of the month. Please pray for that!

The next day we enjoyed breakfast at the hotel where I ordered pancakes for Marvin. He began to devour the pancakes, but about halfway through them, he started to look distressed. I gathered he needed to go to the restroom, so we swiftly made a beeline for the restaurant's bathroom. Poor Marvin started sweating and looked to be having stomach cramps. After using the restroom, he became lethargic and fell asleep on my shoulder. We made our way back to our table, where he continued to sleep. I was concerned that the change in his diet was too much for his digestive system. Thankfully, within an hour he was awake and his normal, playful self.

MY US EMBASSY INTERVIEW

Later that same day, we were picked up by Jameson and taken to Ricardo's guest house to meet up with Lisa, meet Ricardo's wife and children, and see their property. We enjoyed a hearty lunch of eggs and spaghetti noodles, which I would soon learn were staples of the Haitian diet. Marvin's stomach seemed to be feeling much better. While we were there, we discussed upcoming requirements for the adoption process and the need to move Marvin to Chante Lajwa as soon as possible. Legally, Madame Berger had no right to keep him. We discussed our concern about safely getting Marvin out of Delivrans Mwen orphanage and that I would return in March to facilitate this move.

Since I was here this time for my US Embassy interview, we made preparations for my appointment. Since Mike could not attend, I had prepared a power of attorney to enable me to represent Mike in his absence. This embassy appointment was as nerve-racking as any part of the process could be. I sat in their waiting area with what seemed like a hundred Haitians. Finally, it was my turn to approach the window and answer any questions they had about the adoption and our intentions. Those ten minutes of questions seemed like an eternity. When it was finally over, I sighed a huge sigh of relief and headed outside to meet back up with Ricardo, Lisa, and Marvin, who had been waiting nearby.

The next morning, it was already time to go home. I was anxious to see my husband and girls, but with each visit it was becoming increasingly difficult to leave Marvin behind. This bonding trip had proven successful, and Marvin and I were forever linked together. I could tell he was starting to depend on me, which made it all the more difficult to leave. The madame also told me that after I left the last time, Marvin pointed up to the sky and said, "Manman, avyon," which means "Mom, airplane." He was beginning to understand that I came and went, but hopefully, he was also learning to trust that I would always come back for him. I said my tearful goodbyes in the foyer of the orphanage, and Pastor Odson and I headed out, driving along the bumpy, dusty roads to the airport.

CHAPTER 10

Missed Embassy Appointment

I keep my eyes always on the LORD. With him at my right hand, I will not be shaken.
—PSALM 16:8

Facebook Entry: February 1, 2013:
Thank you all for praying for Roselina & Marvin's embassy appointment! Unfortunately, she missed her appointment because Jameson's tire blew out on his way down the mountain, and he was not able to pick her up in time. If you've ever been to Haiti, you understand that it is very hard on cars! :-) We will have to reschedule and try again soon. Bummed, but God's got it under control!

On January 31, 2013, Roselina was scheduled to have her US Embassy appointment with Marvin. As the day approached, I asked on Facebook for prayer that everything would go well with her appointment. The day before, I tried to contact Pastor Odson to confirm that Roselina and Marvin would be ready. After several attempts to phone

Haiti, I received a return call from him, informing me that Roselina was already at the orphanage and would spend the night so she would be ready for her early departure. That was great news to hear. She still seemed to be completely on board with the adoption.

She had already surrendered her parental rights in a Haitian court, but the US Embassy still had to confirm that she was not being coerced in any way. I tried not to worry about the outcome of her appointment, surrendering that fear to God, because only He knew the final outcome.

The day came and went with no news from Lisa or Pastor Odson. I assumed that all went well. Usually, no news from Haiti was good news, but I was to find out that this was not the case. Unfortunately, Jameson blew out two tires in Carrefour and would not receive new tires in time for the appointment. Traffic in Port-au-Prince can be terrible, and it is not like you can call a tow truck to take you to the nearest tire store. I was disappointed, again, but knew that this step would not be holding up our paperwork. God must have had a good reason for the delay.

Lisa suggested I contact the embassy by email, explain to them what happened, and request a new appointment. A few days after my email request to the embassy, I received a new appointment for Roselina and Marvin. They were now scheduled to have their interview on March 20, 2013, almost exactly one year since we first met Marvin. I sent Pastor Odson an email asking him if he would contact Roselina and let her know about her new appointment date. I also asked him to remind Madame Berger that we would be coming soon to move Marvin to the new orphanage.

Facebook Entry: February 21, 2013

Adoption prayer warriors needed again! Please pray that we make it out of Presidential Dispensation soon because we can't go forward until the President signs off on our documents. Also there are some issues with the process that need to be heavily covered in prayer. God knows the need, just ask Him to please straighten the path a little bit so we don't fall off :-) This sweet video was taken by our friends during their December visit. I guess I can add "loves lollipops" to my list of things Marvin likes. :-)

CHAPTER 11

Ransom Request

And now, dear lady, I am not writing you a new command but one we have had from the beginning. I ask that we love one another.
—2 JOHN 1:5

On Sunday, February 10, Mike, Brooke, and I were at his parents' house celebrating the seventy-fifth birthday of a family friend. Mike's parents, Sharon and Jay, were always gracious hosts as we celebrated many occasions and events at their home. As we prepared to gather for dinner, I happened to check my phone for messages. With Kelsey away at school in Birmingham, I tended to be a little anxious about checking my phone. I tried not to be a helicopter parent and I did not contact her too often, but I just wanted to be reachable in case of an emergency.

I noticed that an email from "Makenson" with a subject line of "information" was on my screen. Well, that was interesting, because I did not know anyone named Makenson except for Madame Berger's translator in Haiti. I opened the email and immediately got that familiar sick feeling in the pit of my stomach that accompanies bad news. What did he want from us, and how did he get our contact information? Well, here was what he wanted:

Hi Catie & Mike,

Dear Friends:

It is a really pleasure to write and greet you.

    I'm very agree with you to adopt Marvens in my orphanage in hoping the condition of his life will be improved in your home than in Delivrans Mwen orphanage. However, as I was talking to you concerning my right of the work, I would like to tell you I get Marvens since in the beginning of the 2010 that means 3 years ago. I spent my energy, my nights, some time my money to take care of this child.

    So, before Marvens get out of the Delivrans Mwen to another orphanage it is wiser to pay me my rate which is four thousand dollars US. This the lower amount that I can claim from you.

    I think you will understand this process.
    May God bless you all.

Yours,
Madame Jean Berger

Needless to say, we were a little upset that they were basically holding our son for ransom, for four thousand dollars!! We reeled, "How dare they attempt to extort money out of us!" I had already explained to them on my last visit that we could not and would not pay them to release Marvin. Even if we had wanted to pay them money, it was against the law and considered child trafficking. We were very disappointed to receive the ransom email, but we were not at all surprised. We knew something like this would eventually come to light with Madame Berger and Makenson. We knew deep down that something was going on with them and that they could not be trusted. Too many lies had been told in the past.

I immediately forwarded the email to Lisa and Shawn for their thoughts. We worried as to how we should respond. What were we going to do? How would we get Marvin out of there without a standoff? Lisa had a lot more experience with people in Haiti, and she advised us to not even reply to the email. She then encouraged us, reminding us that Ricardo had a lot of experience with tense situations. We were counting on his expertise to free our son.

A few days later, Shawn and I discussed a possible trip together to move Marvin to Chante Lajwa, sooner rather than later. We needed Shawn's authority, as our church's financial representative for Delivrans Mwen, and his relationship with the orphanage to be able to pull this off. We devised a plan to return to Haiti in a couple of weeks and pay a "surprise visit" to the orphanage. We were very concerned that if the madame knew we were coming, she would remove Marvin from the orphanage and hide him with family or friends. We agreed that we would let Pastor Odson know in advance what we were planning to do and would prayerfully ask him not to tip off Madame Berger. It was ironic that shortly after I received the ransom email, Shawn received an email from an American contact in Haiti who had tried to help with some of the very sick children in Delivrans Mwen orphanage over the holidays. This was what we discovered from her:

Just to let you know about Delivrans Mwen... We brought in a lot of different organizations to try to help them. They have Makenson working there who has been contacting everyone, constantly asking for more and more stuff. He confessed to one group that when the orphanage gets food donations, he shares it with his sister's family. That did not go over very well with those who were donating to help the children! Most who were wanting to

help have withdrawn because they don't want to be har-
assed by Makenson. He has called me repeatedly asking
for food, Christmas gifts for himself, a job because he isn't
satisfied there, etc. I would be willing to help the children,
but am tired of dealing with Makenson! Sorry to unload,
but wanted to make you aware of the situation.

The news made me sick. Deep down I knew kids were
frequently going hungry, but I did not suspect those running
the orphanage were stealing food and supplies intended for
the children. The kids were not getting proper nutrition or
enough food; no wonder so many of them were sick in
December. Not only that, but other organizations were refus-
ing to help because of Makenson's involvement. How much
other aid had backed away that we would never know about?
We knew something had to be done about the situation.

It was more urgent than ever that Shawn and I make a
trip down to Haiti to get to the bottom of this and to move
Marvin. Mike was in the throes of our busy spring landscaping season and coaching Brooke's high school softball team
and would not be able to make this trip. Mike and I offered
to pay for Shawn's trip, and he in return offered to be the
perceived authority needed to move Marvin. We needed
someone who had Madame Berger's trust to be able to insist
we were going to move Marvin, without paying four thousand dollars to do it.

CHAPTER 12

Operation Rescue Marvin

May the God of hope fill you with all joy and peace
as you trust in him, so that you may overflow with
hope by the power of the Holy Spirit.
—ROMANS 5:13

In March, Shawn and I drove to Atlanta to head to Haiti. To save money, Shawn graciously agreed to fly a discount airline. As on my previous trip, the only option to arrive in Haiti early in the day was to stay overnight in Fort Lauderdale and catch the early flight out, but even with the hotel expense the savings were significant. I had only one prior experience with this airline, and three out of my four flight legs were delayed. We knew it was a risk, but we thought the cost savings was worth it. Upon arriving in Atlanta, we discovered that our first flight to Fort Lauderdale was delayed. Surprise, surprise! We were hoping this was not the precedent for the rest of the trip.

The last time I took this airline, my flight was so delayed that by the time I arrived at my hotel it was after midnight, and I had to leave the next morning at 5:00 a.m. It just was not worth a hundred plus dollars for the little bit of sleep I was able to get, so I adamantly told Shawn that I was going to sleep in the airport. Shawn was having none of it and booked himself a budget motel for the night.

When we arrived in Fort Lauderdale, it was so late that Shawn missed the last shuttle offered by this hotel. As we disembarked the plane, I asked the gate attendant if I could sleep in the terminal. He informed me that I could sleep outside by the ticketing counters, but that the terminals would close at 2:00 a.m. Bummer! There was no carpet by the ticketing counters, and the seats were very close to the doors. Maybe this was not such a good idea after all. Shawn called the motel and confirmed they had an extra room for me. I guess I had to stay in another budget airport hotel. Why was it that I could shower with a five-gallon bucket in Haiti, but I did not want to stay in a budget hotel in America? It was funny how my mind would rationalize things. Since we had missed the last shuttle, we had to catch a cab, which cost me another twenty dollars both ways, because we found out upon arrival at the motel that the morning shuttle did not start until 6:00 a.m. I decided once and for all that this budget airline was becoming not so budget.

The next morning, we thankfully arrived on time in Port-au-Prince. When we reached baggage claim, we called Pastor Odson and he said he was on his way. You learn quickly that in Haiti, "on their way" was not necessarily relative to how much time it would take to get there. We did not know at the time, but Pastor Odson had to take Abeline, a sick little girl from the orphanage, to the hospital for her latent tuberculosis treatment. We were sad to find out she had tested positive for tuberculosis.

Traffic was especially bad in Port-au-Prince that morning, because it had poured rain the night before. When it rained hard in Haiti, it wreaked havoc on the area because it was not equipped for that amount of water runoff. They do not have storm sewers and retention ponds like we do, so everything runs on the surface, flooding anything along the way. We take these things for granted but imagine a torrential downpour in a city with hills and no natural or man-made way to channel water. It was a huge mess.

When Pastor Odson finally arrived, we made our necessary trip to the Mega Mart to pick up some groceries and supplies for the orphanage. We had no intention of showing up empty-handed, especially with the task at hand of taking Marvin with us and showing up unannounced. When we arrived, we found out that Mega Mart was closing soon for renovations, so there was not much on the shelves to choose from. We picked up a few things and then headed to the Star 2000 grocery store instead and managed to completely fill the grocery cart with food and supplies.

Next, we headed to the local neighborhood market to buy rice, beans, and cooking oil. This local market was a small room, maybe ten foot by twenty foot, with an ordering window upfront. This was my first visit to a local store. I had never been beyond the Mega Mart. When the people found out we were placing a large order, they allowed us to enter the store itself. The small market was a mishmash of boxes, products stacked in the middle of the floor, trash strewn about the aisles, broken cartons, expired food, etc. Using Pastor Odson to translate, we managed to order huge sacks of beans, rice, flour, large jugs of cooking oil, and even a few toiletries. After we placed our order, we exited the store and waited by Pastor Odson's SUV for them to bring everything out and load it up. Now, we were finally able to head to the orphanage. Of course, I was very anxious to see my son and get this transfer over with as soon as possible. I tried not to play out potential scenarios in my head.

On the way to Delivrans Mwen, we reiterated to Pastor Odson our purpose and why we were coming unannounced. We explained to him that we feared Madame Berger would hide Marvin with Makenson until we agreed to pay her for her services. He shared with us that he was aware of Makenson causing problems, and that since Shawn had received the email about Makenson running off other churches with his strong-arm tactics, he had fired him from the orphanage. That was a huge relief to hear. I was especially relieved that he would not be a part of these negotiations. He always seemed to "stir the pot" and make things more difficult. I said a silent prayer thanking God for removing that obstacle before our necessary visit.

INITIAL NEGOTIATIONS

When we first arrived, I stayed by the vehicle to protect the food items as Shawn, Pastor Odson, and some of the older children unloaded everything. When I finally made it into the front room, I spotted Marvin in the mix of children. He greeted me with the biggest smile, and I managed to weave my way through the other kids to get to him. I wanted to hug all of them, but I especially wanted to wrap Marvin up in a huge hug. Even though we had arrived unannounced, Madame Berger seemed happy to see both of us. She gave big hugs and then disappeared into her room to properly dress for company.

We spent the rest of the afternoon playing with the kids as Pastor Odson had to return to the hospital to pick up Abilene. As the hours wore on and Pastor Odson did not return, I wondered if and when we were ever going to have our meeting with Madame Berger. We helped the little ones eat their lunch, and Marvin was the first to clean his plate.

We would later observe that Marvin would always be a member of the clean plate club.

Marvin (with the sticker on his head) and friends eating every drop

Praying that our negotiations would go smoothly and that we would be bringing Marvin with us, we had made prior arrangements for Ricardo to pick us up at 3:30 p.m. at the orphanage. As the hours passed by, I realized we would not be ready by then. Shawn called Ricardo, and we agreed that we would call him as soon as we were ready. Remember, though, we did not want to be out in Port-au-Prince at night.

I was so relieved when Pastor Odson finally returned late in the afternoon. Traffic was terrible again and delayed his arrival. We immediately called a meeting with the four of us: Shawn, myself, Pastor Odson, and Madame Berger. The first revelation of the meeting was Pastor Odson relaying that Madame had reduced her "ransom fee" to $1,000. We had agreed in advance that Shawn would do most of the negotiating. First, he explained that he was pleased with what we saw at the orphanage upon arrival. The kids were clean, the house was clean, we knew how hard she worked to run this orphanage. He reiterated that we could not pay her because it was against the law, and that we were very grateful for all her love and care for Marvin.

She was visibly angry, loud, and did not want to budge on her demands. She talked about how she never got to see her ailing mom who lived far away. Shawn told her that when our intern arrived in April or May, she might be able to have some time off to see her mom. I wondered how this related to moving Marvin, but I could sympathize with her point. She was grasping at straws for something, anything, to extort money out of us. I was getting visibly frustrated at this point. We discussed the future plans for the orphanage, and how far they had come in the last eighteen months since our church had gotten involved. At this point, Shawn asked me to leave the room for a few moments, and I agreed. We had not discussed this previously, so I was not sure what he had planned. I reluctantly left and headed out to the back steps where children proceed to fight for a spot on my lap.

After the longest ten minutes of my life had passed, Shawn retrieved me from my child "dog pile" on the back steps. While we walked back to the room where we were meeting, he said that we were done, and we were ready to move forward with taking Marvin with us today. What?? What was said? Shawn refused to ever tell me what was said during those ten minutes, but it must have been pretty powerful. We reentered the meeting room, and I profusely thanked Madame Berger for all she had done for Marvin. Despite the situation, we hugged and she doted on Marvin while he was in my arms. I did not doubt that she cared for Marvin, but I was sure that she saw us as a monetary opportunity and felt entitled to compensation.

FREE AT LAST!

Shawn called Ricardo to come get us, but he informed us it was going to take at least an hour for him to reach us. I changed Marvin into pajamas and the new shoes that we brought for him and started the process of saying goodbye to everyone. The shoes I brought for Marvin were light-up shoes, and the children discovered this as I was holding him in my arms. They proceeded to beat his feet to make them light up. In hindsight, this was probably not the best purchase for the situation.

The sun was setting, and Ricardo was still not there. There was no way to avoid it, but we realized that we would be driving through the streets of Port-au-Prince at night. I silently prayed for our safety and for Ricardo's speedy arrival. I was still uneasy, because I knew this was not finished until we were safely inside Ricardo's vehicle. As we said our final goodbyes and Madame Berger was crying, I felt a small tinge of guilt for taking Marvin away from the only home he could remember. He would receive much better care and love at his new orphanage, but this would still be a huge life change for our little guy, and I would not be there to walk him through it. The struggles of international adoption were not for the faint of heart.

Ricardo and Jameson finally arrived, and Shawn, Marvin, and I quickly climbed into the backseat. The four of us hugged with joy (and maybe a few tears on my part). We hurriedly told Ricardo, "Get out of here quick!" We did not get far before we were stuck in major traffic. We dropped Ricardo off to run an errand, and then were thankful to stop in Petionville at a local restaurant for dinner. Ricardo joined back up with us midway during the meal. I was sure the locals were very curious as to why two blans (white people) were out for dinner with a Haitian child in his pajamas and two friends at night. We must have been quite the sight. It also did not take me long to figure out that Marvin's stomach was not feeling well (he made three bathroom trips at the restaurant alone) and thank goodness I brought a hefty supply of diaper wipes with me, as usual. As my friends know, I usually have a wipe for everything and every reason.

After what seemed like the longest day of my whole life, we safely pulled up to Ricardo's gated guest house. We visited briefly with his wife and children, and then I took Marvin up to ready him for bed. With access to Wi-Fi, this was my first chance to really speak to Mike and tell him the good news of the day. We were able to Skype on our iPad, and Marvin loved getting to see his "Papi's" face. Papi is "Daddy" in Creole. I was so excited that Marvin would be heading to a new home with ample food and loving care. I fell asleep quickly that night and did not even worry that the windows of the guest house did not have screens. I thought how I would most likely be mosquito dinner throughout the night, but with the most precious little boy sound asleep next to me, nothing else mattered.

Facebook Entries: March 7, 2013

Today is a big day on the adoption front. Can't go into details yet, but please pray for discernment, protection, and God's favor!! Please keep praying that we exit the President's office soon, some people have been there for months :-(

Today was exhausting, but God is always good and it went better than expected. Arrived in Haiti today & loved every minute with my boy!! More details soon, please pray for safe travels tomorrow, Marvin & my first road trip together. :-)

OVER THE MOUNTAIN

The next morning, after Jameson made some repairs to the black SUV we would be traveling in, we all loaded up to make the long journey to the Chante Lajwa orphanage. The cook who would be traveling with us, Jasmine, had arrived. She rode up front with Jameson while Shawn, Marvin, and I rode in the back. We had to travel through Port-au-Prince to get to Camatin, and we stopped at the Star 2000 market for juice and sodas. We also stopped at a furniture store to buy a mattress and box spring for Marvin. I hoped I brought enough cash for this unplanned purchase.

We decided it was important for Marvin's manman to accompany us on this trip, since this would likely be the last time she would see Marvin for months or longer. She would not have the funds to travel to Camatin and visit, although I was not sure how much she visited him while he was in Port-au-Prince. After the Star 2000, we picked up Roselina on a designated street corner. She was thrilled to see all of us.

As usual, there was a lot of traffic in the city. In my past, I had spent several years commuting in Atlanta, and I thought I had seen bad traffic. However, Port-au-Prince and sur-rounding areas could easily rival anything I had ever seen before. The biggest problem in Haiti was that they have no traffic lanes, few traffic control devices such as stop signs or traffic signals, and few if any traffic laws. Drivers create their own lanes, and when they come to a standstill, the only way to clear the jam is to have the police arrive and force someone to back up. They would rather sit there all day and honk and yell than be the gracious one to back up. Of course, you would have to get the people behind you to agree as well, and without authority intervention, that just does not happen.

During the trip, Roselina told us that her brother had recently passed away. Apparently, locals found her brother dead on the beach and they were not sure what had happened to him. I pray it wasn't foul play, but Haiti can be a very dangerous place. Sadly, he was only thirty-two. A few years after Marvin came home with us, another of his uncles was murdered, and another died in a traffic accident. Life expectancy is much shorter in Haiti.

Since Marvin still had a very upset stomach, we made a stop at one of the few gas stations we would pass on the way. Unfortunately, the bathroom was closed for some reason. Marvin was amazing and was able to keep from going at this time. As we started up the mountain road, the SUV began to overheat from the extreme conditions Haiti puts on vehicles. We pulled over to the side of the rural road, and Roselina and Jasmine took Marvin, and a pack of diaper wipes, to a nearby home to ask if he could use their bathroom. I thought it would be best if I did not tag along. The neighborhood children were already waving and calling out "blan!" to get our attention. I was sure we were somewhat of an unusual sight, especially in the rural areas. The people at the house were very nice, and gave Jasmine a large jug of water to cool off our vehicle.

After about half an hour, we proceeded to make our way up into the mountains. Not much further into our journey, though, the SUV started smoking. We were forced to stop on a short, straight stretch of the road. Jameson pulled over as far as he could to the right, half in the roadway and half in the sloped ditch area. The mountain roads here were very treacherous. Drivers flew around corners at rapid speeds, honking as they went to alert oncoming vehicles that they were in the curve. It was only my second experience with Haitian mountain roads, and now we were unsafely stuck on the side of the road for who knew how long. Thankfully, though, God was in the details. We happened to break down about thirty feet from a roadside latrine. It was built of three sides of corrugated metal, a huge hole dug in the ground, and a cinder block "toilet" of sorts, built up to sit on. I had no idea why it was there, but I was beyond grateful. Poor Marvin needed that latrine several times each hour. After he came home and was tested for every ailment under the sun, we discovered Marvin had antibodies for hepatitis A. This means that at some point he had the food-borne illness. When we were there in March, he was probably recovering from his acute attack of hepatitis A, but thankfully you can never get it again.

STRANDED AND SCARED

As Jameson and Shawn assessed the vehicle situation, they discovered that a transmission hose had burst. Shawn had brought some basic tools with him and was able to cut the burst end of the hose off, but when they tried to reattach the hose, it was just a bit too short. They tried so hard, but that hose was determined not to cooperate. We eventually attracted a few locals who wanted to see what was going on and if they could help. At this point, Jameson called Ricardo to send us a mechanic, but the mechanic would be traveling through Port-au-Prince during rush hour traffic. It would be hours before he could arrive.

One of the positives of Marvin not feeling well was that he did not want to do anything but sit in my lap. We tried to pass the time in the vehicle with snacks, the iPad, and just

Our SUV with the dump truck in front

hanging out. We were very grateful that we were in the shade of the mountain trees. We were doing our best to celebrate these small kindnesses—until a huge dump truck broke

Hanging out on the side of the road for hours

down in front of us and started rolling backward toward us! Shawn quickly ordered us all out of the vehicle. The dump truck stopped for good about fifty yards ahead of us, but we could not wait safely in the SUV anymore. If the emergency brake failed on the dump truck, it would go careening down the mountain road and take us with it over the edge. That was not exactly what I had in mind for the afternoon, so we gladly packed up our backpack of stuff and moved across the road.

With our little breakdown party safely on the other side of the road, Shawn, Marvin, and I hung out on a pile of gravel, and the Haitians were hanging out with some of the locals. The only upside to not being able to hang out in the vehicle was that we were closer to the latrine. As the hours wore on, we tried to pass the time playing with the few little toys that I brought for Marvin, but he was content to just hang out in my lap.

Shawn and I discussed what our plan B would be if we did not make it off this mountain before dark. On the right side of the road was a steep, wooded hill with what appeared to be a foot path. We discussed trekking up a small trail into the mountain and hunkering down for the night, but I sure prayed it would not come to that. I am not a huge fan of insects, and spending the night in the woods with no shelter was not on my bucket list.

After about five hours, the mechanics finally arrived as it was getting dark. To my surprise, two of them came on one motorcycle, and they were carrying their tools in a pink, little girl's backpack. In Haiti, you use what you can get your hands on. Unfortunately, they did not bring a flashlight, but thankfully Shawn had one with him. I decided that we should call Shawn "MacGyver" from now on. I was pretty sure he had everything you could need in that small backpack. As a fireman/medic, he even had a birthing kit because, "You just never know!"

The mechanics worked for quite some time, but after repairing the hose they still could not get the vehicle running. At one point, one of the guys walked down the mountain to purchase transmission fluid. Thankfully, people who lived along the road stocked auto parts and supplies for this very purpose. The mechanics then needed to pour the transmission fluid into the vehicle but did not have a funnel. I pulled a little "MacGyver" of my own and created a funnel from a magazine I had in my bag. We finally got the vehicle started, and everyone cheered and praised God at the sweet sound of the engine running.

REPAIRED AND BACK ON
THE ROAD—PRAISE GOD

As we started back up the mountain with our mechanics following behind, the Haitians started singing worship songs in Creole. We all lifted our hands in praise that we were back on the road. This was a sight I would never forget. In the comfort of my home, and life back in the States, I often forget to praise the One who really deserves the glory. This was a lesson for me on fully relying on God in all my circumstances.

We arrived at Chante Lajwa in the mountains well after dark. The kids were very interested in us, but they were already getting ready for bed. Since visitors were encouraged to bring or pay for a separate cook, so as to not burden the regular cooks, Jasmine immediately started to prepare a meal for us. Roselina and I went upstairs to the guest quarters to get Marvin washed up for bed. With so little space in my suitcase, I had brought only one bath towel, which the three of us shared. She did not have any pajamas either, so I gave her mine. It was much cooler in the mountains than it was in

Port-au-Prince, so that ice cold shower was quite a shock. We went downstairs and ate a wonderful meal of spaghetti noodles and spicy slaw. Marvin ate like a champion, and we quickly rushed him off to bed. It had been a very long day for all of us.

Poor Marvin woke up at least six times throughout the night with stomach problems, but he never once had an accident, and he did not complain. I was not going to get much sleep, but I cherished every moment of being able to care for him. His manman slept through every episode. I figured she knew I was there and was handling the situation. She probably had not had a good night's sleep in a real bed in a very long time. For all I knew, she may have never slept in a real bed with a mattress.

DAY TRIP TO JACMEL

The next day after breakfast we loaded up to head to Jacmel to buy more supplies. We stopped at a pharmacy first, and while we were there, they lost power. Haiti's power grid is quite unstable, so I imagine that was a common occurrence for them. Jameson then parked in an old gas station that had been turned into an auto parts store. He wanted to get a few things in case they had more car trouble.

While we were hanging out, Marvin appeared uncomfortable and said that he needed to use the restroom again. Roselina had walked away, so Shawn and I looked around for a possible bathroom. Haiti is not like the United States where you can find public restrooms almost anywhere. We walked toward what looked like a service station, our group sticking out like a sore thumb, for sure. We asked if they had a restroom, but they did not. We ventured further down the road, and by now, Marvin was getting desperate. We saw a nice older lady sweeping outside a small apartment complex, so we approached her. She was so kind to let these three strangers into her home to use her bathroom. I was mortified that Marvin would leave an unpleasant smell throughout her apartment, because we had to walk through her bedroom to reach the bathroom. Thankfully, he only had to pee! We thanked her profusely, waved, and continued our journey.

When we arrived back at the vehicle's previous location, it was gone! We wondered where in the world they had taken it. I had brief images of the movie *Open Water*, where two scuba divers get left behind by their charter boat. As we looked around searching for the familiar SUV, Jameson came driving up. He was worried he had lost us in Jacmel. We were all relieved to be reunited. We headed back up the mountain toward the orphanage. We broke down again on the way, but thankfully we were smart this time and brought the mechanic with us. After some brief tinkering, we were on our way once again.

We spent the rest of the day getting to know the children in Chante Lajwa who would become Marvin's friends for the foreseeable future. We had no idea it would be fourteen long months before we could bring Marvin home. We knew the process could take a long time, but we thought the end was much closer than it really was. These kids would be his family. I was very thankful that he seemed to be making fast friends with the other boys. One of the older boys wanted to hold Marvin's hand and show him around, but Marvin was not ready for that. We got his bed set up in the boy's room and spent time exploring the orphanage and the grounds together. Chante Lajwa is located in a rural, mountainous area, with lots of space to safely play outside. They even had a small playground onsite. This would be a much-welcomed change from living within the confines of a two-story home with a concrete back yard.

Marvin ate lunch with all the children. It warmed my heart to see the older girls show him where his seat would be and help pull him up to the table. Before all the children sat down, they stood behind their chairs and prayed together over their food. He was going to be just fine. Later that evening, we ate a delicious meal consisting of Haitian meatballs. Against my better judgment, Roselina loaded him up with the meatballs and hot sauce. Of course, his stomach was upset four times in the wee hours, and he burped those darn meatballs in my face all night long. I also discovered that his birth manman has full-on conversations in her sleep. She also liked to talk on the phone in the middle of the night. I wondered to myself why these conversations could not wait until daylight hours.

MOUNTAIN CHURCH AND SETTLING IN

On Sunday, we attended the little local church just up the hill from the orphanage. It was about a four-hour-long service, and Marvin quickly fell asleep on the bench with his head in my lap. I did not mind a long service, but the bench was basically a two-by-six seat with a horizontal piece of wood in our back. When turned around they could be used as school desks, which was why the horizontal piece was there. Not accustomed to sitting like this for hours on end, I was very uncomfortable, and my rear end was feeling it. About midway through the service, I was just overcome with the emotion of the whole situation. As I said before, I am very tenderhearted, and I just could not stop the tears from flowing. Sometimes the greatness of God's glory just consumes me.

I left Marvin in Shawn's lap and had to step out of the service to compose myself. Sometimes that part of who I am can be so embarrassing. I walked down the hill to the orphanage by myself, my chest heaving up and down with uncontrolled tears. I just could not fathom how God chose me to be the mother of the precious child that lay sleeping in my lap. I mourned all the things I was missing in his life while we waited for what seemed like an eternity to bring him home. I asked God, "Why does it have to take so long? Is he going to be okay emotionally, when all this is said and done?" I pleaded for protection of his little heart, and that he would settle well into his new home.

After I splashed some cold water on my face and was able to stop the tears, I hiked back up the hill to the church service. I felt terrible that I had missed hearing Shawn speak in front of the congregation. When the service was complete, we all walked back down the hill to the orphanage. Two of the older girls came alongside Marvin, and they each took a hand. God knew I needed that glimpse of hope and reassurance at that moment. My heart needed some concrete comfort, and He provided it through the loving hands of two little girls.

After church, Jameson gave Marvin and some of the other boys a haircut. They did not own an electric clipper, so they strapped a razor blade to a small, black comb using a rubber band. We would later discover that most of the boys had ringworm on their scalps. At the time, I had no idea what the little white spots were on most of the boys' heads. The makeshift razor was ingenious, and the boys looked so handsome after their haircuts. I could also see Marvin soaking up some much-needed time with a male authority figure. His whole life he had been cared for by women, with only limited contact with caring, adult men. Jameson was cool and had a great rapport with all of the children. I could already tell he was going to be a blessing during his trips to the orphanage.

SAYING GOODBYE, AGAIN

Not too long after church, it was time to make our way back down the mountain to Port-au-Prince. Our trip was coming to a close, but I was not ready to say goodbye. We walked into the boys' bedroom to find Marvin showing them some of his toys. It was a precious sight, seeing them all gathered around the bed. The Lord whispered to my heart that he would be fine. Jameson told us it was time to go, and now would be a good time, while he was distracted with the other boys. I asked Jameson to tell Marvin that I would miss him and would be back soon. I broke into tears mid-sentence, so I gave Marvin a quick kiss and a hug goodbye and left the room.

As soon as I left the room, the tears started to flow again. Doubts flooded my mind. "How could I leave him here when he had been here for only two days?" I did what I had to do, though. We loaded our things in the SUV and headed down the dirt road. I left a huge chunk of my heart behind in Haiti that day. That was probably one of the hardest things I have ever done in my life.

As we entered the main road from the orphanage drive-way, Jameson realized he had forgotten to pray before our trip began. He promptly stopped the SUV in the road and prayed in Creole over our trip. We all made easy conversation even with our limited Creole and their limited English. We all had a good laugh as we passed the broken-down dump truck that had been part of our roadside adventure just a few days earlier. It was still stranded on the side of the mountain. Once we arrived back in Port-au-Prince, we asked Jameson to drop us off at the Delivrans Mwen orphanage. I was tense about seeing Madame Berger again, but we needed to check on some things before we left the country.

As soon as we arrived, the children were overwhelmed to see us again. Some of them were getting a bath, and little Abeline had gotten soap in her eyes, so she was wandering around wet and crying. I scooped her up in search of a towel. Once again, it broke my heart that these precious little ones have no one to comfort them during life's hurts. I was busy getting her dressed when we heard a knock at the steel front door. We assumed it was Pastor Odson, but it was actually our driver from our previous mission trips to Haiti. He was a wonderful man with a tender heart and a great ability to navigate the dangerous streets of Haiti. Shawn and I were both thrilled to see him. Pastor Odson had sent him to pick us up and take us to the guest house. We visited for a little bit longer with the children, and I shared photos of Marvin, his new home, and friends with Madame Berger. She genuinely seemed excited to see those photos. She kissed the photo on my phone, and then proceeded to pass the phone around for the other children to see.

We attempted in our limited Creole to tell them goodbye and that we loved them. As we did, one of the little girls started to cry and cling to us. The driver explained that she was begging us to take her with us. We wished we could break them all out of the cycle of poverty and orphanage living. We gently pried her away as we stepped outside to leave. She attempted to get in the car with us, but we had to physically take her back inside the orphanage and get them to lock the door. Once again, our heartstrings were torn apart. I uttered under my breath, "Come soon, Jesus, come soon."

Shawn wanted to make a quick visit to see the little boys who had stolen his heart on his early trips to Haiti, so the driver drove us down the street to a little tent settlement. We wove our way through identical blue tarp tents in search of his family. Miraculously, we found their tent, and the boys' mom greeted us with open arms. The younger boy, Tyre, suddenly appeared from around the corner and jumped into Shawn's arms. He was very excited to see him. Then the driver showed up, probably worried that we had gotten lost. Finally, Wesley arrived, and Shawn got to hug his favorite Haitian boy. Thankfully, later down the road, Shawn was able to help Wesley and Tyre enroll in the Compassion International child sponsorship program. Through this program, they receive nutrition, medical care, educational support, and Christ-centered guidance.

Shawn and the boys

MISSION ACCOMPLISHED

Once we returned and settled into the guest house, I attempted to reach Mike and the girls through Skype. The Internet was acting up, so I did not get to have a long, detailed conversation, but at least they knew we were safely back in Port-au-Prince. We ate another wonderful meal prepared by the guest house staff. We had the honor of meeting Weston, another missionary who was staying in the guest house. He spoke Creole, Spanish, and English, and had adopted three Haitian children himself.

After dinner, Shawn, Pastor Odson, Weston, and Pastor Charles, who ran the guest house, left for an evening church service. I could not muster the energy to go and quickly settled in for the night. I had gotten very little sleep over the past few days because of Marvin's stomach problems, so this tired, forty-something mom attempted to go to bed early that night. Unfortunately, sleep eluded me as the events of the last few days swirled around in my head. I already missed Marvin terribly. Thankfully, sleep finally overtook me around 1:00 a.m.

Facebook Entry: March 11, 2013

Headed home today. It was so hard to say goodbye yesterday, but we got Marvin settled into his new home. I cannot wait to bring him home!! We spent 6 hours broken down on the side of the mountain Friday. Poor Marvin had a very upset tummy all weekend, but God is in the details…we broke down right next to a latrine!! We finally made it after dark. When we left, Marvin was showing his toys to his new roomies. We are forever in Uncle Shawn's debt!

The next morning, we ate and packed up our things for our departure. Shawn's friend, Micha, joined us during the ride to the airport. Shawn had met him during one of his Samaritan's Purse mission trips and wanted a chance to say a quick hello. It was nice to meet him, and he made my day by asking if I was finished with school yet. I laughed hard and told him he was my new best friend. The line at the airport was unusually long, but we boarded our flight with no delays. We finally made it back to Atlanta and drove to Knoxville in a torrential downpour. Thankfully, we made it back to our homes safely, and resumed our lives filled with daily activities. I missed Marvin dearly, and prayed this process would somehow speed up, and the pitter-patter of little toddler feet would soon fill our home.

Facebook Entry: March 16, 2013

One year ago today, our family fell in love with the most precious boy...our son Marvin. He wrapped my neck in the biggest hug ever and stole our hearts! Praying we exit dispensation soon & that his birth mom's embassy appointment goes well next Wednesday the 20th.

Facebook Entry: March 20, 2013

Embassy appointment for Marvin & Roselina is complete! So grateful, thank You, Lord. Please keep praying we will exit dispensation very soon! The file is stuck until it comes out. Thank you all for your prayers!!

DISPENSATION REQUIREMENT

Haiti had several requirements that each adoption must meet. The adoptive parents must be of a certain age, they must not have any biological children, and they must be married a certain number of years. If you did not meet all of these requirements, you had to have special presidential permission or dispensation to be allowed to adopt. Since we had biological children, we were required to go to presidential dispensation. Once the president approved your case file, the approvals would be published in the newspaper. On March 19, 2013, seventy names were published that exited dispensation, but sadly Marvin's name was not listed.

The months wore on and on as we waited for our paperwork to exit dispensation. Finally, on June 25, 2013, his name was published, and we finally exited dispensation. Thank the Lord, one more hurdle had been successfully crossed.

CHAPTER 13

Mountain Visit

*I have always been mindful of your unfailing love
and have lived in reliance on your faithfulness.*
—PSALM 26:3

I n late July 2013, I scheduled another visit to see Marvin. I
missed him terribly, and four months was just too long
for this mother's heart to bear. We had been receiving fairly
regular updates from Chante Lajwa, but that just could not
replace actually spending time with our son. Once again, I
flew into Port-au-Prince and prayed this journey up and
over the mountain would be less memorable. Jameson
picked me up from the airport, and we headed to the
orphanage in Camatin. As soon as we pulled up, the kids
gathered around the entrance to the home and greeted us
with big smiles. I could see Marvin peeking out from behind
one of the older girls. As soon as I got out of the car, he came
running into my open arms.

We enjoyed several days together, just hanging out. We
played games, went on adventures, and ate wonderful
Haitian food. Marvin and I stayed up on the second floor,
where the guests stay. Each day he was allowed to bring up
one friend to spend time with us, and I enjoyed getting to
know some of his new friends. Marvin was a completely dif-

ferent child on this trip. His true boisterous, funny, energetic personality was finally showing through. I got to know his nanny, Madeline, and I could immediately see they shared a special bond. One day I watched as she sat Indian style on the floor playing a game with some of the kids and staff. Marvin came up behind her and was hanging on her back, leaning over her shoulder to see what was going on. I could tell she loved him, and he loved her. What a blessing this relationship was to all of us. As thankful as we were for this wonderful care he was receiving, it was also hard at the same time as feelings of jealousy and injustice tugged at my heart. It was not directed at her at all, but it was directed at the process and the time it was taking to bring him home.

The second day we were there, we went into town to buy new clothes and shoes for Marvin. Madeline said he needed new church and play clothes, as he was rapidly growing. I wished I had known; I could have loaded up from home, but I was up for the adventure ahead. Marvin seemed to truly enjoy the car ride to Jacmel as well as the hustle and bustle of the outdoor market. There were many tents set up for people to sell all sorts of goods. We ended up buying him the cutest blue dress shirt, jeans, school socks, dress shoes, play shoes, and more. He was going to look so handsome. To purchase all these items, which were not any less expensive there, I had to get money from an ATM. That was a little stressful, but I was thankful, again, that I took French in high school as I navigated the questions on the machine.

The next few days were spent bonding and hanging out. As usual, I had some memorable experiences on my visit. One day, Marvin and I were strolling through the lower level of the orphanage when a huge rat came flying around the corner chasing a smaller rat. Marvin freaked out and I did too! There was a cute baby goat running around as well, but he was pooping everywhere, so Jameson picked up the goat and pretended to chase Marvin around with it. Looking back, this may have been a precursor to Marvin's fear of animals. One of the older girls wanted to show me her chickens, so we went out back and checked out the chicken coop. She proceeded to tell me that one chicken in particular was sick. As we ate chicken for dinner that evening, I prayed I was not eating the sick chicken, but I was pretty sure I was.

Before the trip I was given details of my visit, such as who would pick me up from the airport, where I would be staying, and how much money I needed to bring. However, I must have missed the communication stating that I would be receiving only one meal a day while staying at the orphanage. On all prior trips to Haiti, I typically ate two times a day, so I was prepared with enough snacks and granola bars to cover that third meal. This trip, my extra supply was rapidly dwindling, especially since I was sharing the snacks with Marvin. Of course, I survived, but vowed to be more prepared for the next visit.

Marvin was really funny about sharing me on this trip. As we would walk hand in hand through the orphanage, other children would come up and grab my free hand. Marvin was having none of that, as he would fuss loudly in Creole at the other child saying, "Mwen manman!" which means, "My mom!" I told Marvin he had to share but was secretly thankful for this attachment and possessiveness.

The few days I was there went by entirely too fast. I pleaded in my prayers for the whole adoption process to be over soon, for Marvin to be safe in our arms for good. I was very thankful that he was doing so much better and thriving in his new home, but I was ready for this emotional roller coaster to end. As we said our goodbyes, little did I know it would be *ten more months* before I would hold him in my arms and love on him again! On my final day, Marvin and I said our goodbyes. I placed him in the capable arms of Madeline, once again leaving a huge chunk of my heart in Haiti.

After my return home to Knoxville, our waiting game continued. Our sweet friends hosted an amazing adoption shower for our family. Since our girls were so much older than Marvin, we had long since passed on all toddler items we would need once Marvin came home. Family and friends gifted us with all the necessities we would need on his arrival. They had the most precious t-shirts made for Marvin with sayings like "Don't tell my parents, I don't look a thing like them," "I grew in my Mommy's heart, not under it," "Worth the Wait," and "I was born in my Mama's heart." These were the best and Marvin wore one home the day he arrived in the States. It was a relief knowing Marvin would be wrapped in love once he arrived home. We knew he would be treated like he had always been a part of our family.

Our amazing friends who threw us an adoption shower

Our family at the adoption shower

CHAPTER 14

Almost Home

*Consider it pure joy, my brothers and sisters, whenever
you face trials of many kinds, because you know that
the testing of your faith produces perseverance.*
—JAMES 1:2,3

The days since my last visit turned into months, and the
months threatened to turn into a year. We really could
not financially afford to take another trip to Haiti to visit
Marvin, and it was breaking our hearts. We had successfully
exited the court system in Haiti, and Marvin had received his
Haitian passport.

Back in February 2014, Marvin had to undergo some
blood tests to make sure he could pass his visa appointment.
That included screening for anemia, sickle cell disease, other
hemoglobin disorders, syphilis, and HIV. I was thankful that
all these tests came back clear for Marvin, but sad that I was
not there to comfort him when they had to draw blood.
However, I was very grateful for people like Jameson,
Ricardo, and Madeline who often handled this type of
appointment for all the children being adopted. You could
tell they genuinely loved and cared for the children. I could
see it any time Marvin interacted with them; he loved and
trusted them unconditionally.

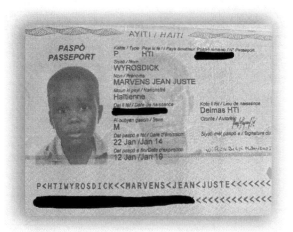

Marvin's Haitian passport

The adoption decree was final in Haiti, and our huge case file finally arrived at the US Embassy. Unfortunately, on March 3, 2014, we received an email from the US Embassy that we were missing a particular document. Apparently, the Court of Jacmel's abstract minutes had arrived at the embassy without translation. We checked our paperwork and were positive it had been submitted correctly, but there was either something missing or something they did not like about our submission. At this point, we were willing to do whatever was needed to make them happy and move this forward. It was quite frustrating to be held up by our own government at the very end of the process. A month later, we successfully submitted that missing document.

Nine months after my last visit, we finally received good news. On April 22, 2014, we received an email from the US Embassy Adoption Unit that our I-604 was complete. This was amazing news! An I-604 is when the US Department of State has made a determination on a child for adoption. It contains all the information about the child up for adoption, the petitioners (that's us), whether the child fits the suitability criteria for adoption, if the petitioner fingerprints are valid, why the intended child was an orphan, and if all the necessary evidence has been presented. Now that this document was complete, we could apply for his visa interview, which we scheduled to take place at the US Embassy in Port-au-Prince on May 7. A group of adoptive parents (adopting from Chante Lajwa) planned to be in Haiti that day to accompany several of the children to their visa appointments. They were in the process of bringing their children home and were just a few weeks ahead of us in the process. We had been communicating in a group email and through Lisa. We were happy to hear this as Marvin needed to have additional blood drawn during this appointment, and it was nice knowing a mom or dad going through the same process would be there to comfort him. They were kind to share photos of Marvin devouring a meal of spicy chicken after the appointment. He still loves spicy chicken to this day.

We were so close, I could almost feel him being home and a forever part of our family. It was the strangest feeling, waiting for a child who was already born, versus waiting to birth a child. It was so heart wrenching, because I felt like I was missing out on so much of Marvin's life during the waiting process. These were the times when I would really have to lean into God and trust that He was holding our son in His hands and that everything would happen in His perfect timing.

We had been advised by Ricardo not to purchase airline tickets until after the visa appointment was complete. As much as adoptive parents want to rush over there as soon as possible, there was no guarantee that the visa appointment would be successful.

We were in contact with two other families who were adopting girls from the same orphanage and had discussed traveling together, to make it easier on the ministry in Haiti.

Every trip from Port-au-Prince over the mountain to Chante Lajwa was a significant expense in fuel, wear and tear on their vehicles, and labor expense in people accompanying the group. After a few text messages back and forth, we booked our travel for Wednesday, May 14, with a return date of Friday evening, May 16. We were still taking a risk booking our tickets before the visa was approved, but it was one we were willing to take. We were beyond excited to actually have an airline ticket purchased for all of us. I felt like Marvin's one-way ticket home was the golden ticket! We were cutting it close for sure, because on May 13, 2014, Marvin's visa was finally picked up by Ricardo. We were grateful the finish line was in sight!

HOMECOMING IS ALMOST HERE

I excitedly started to make the final arrangements to bring our son home. When I purchased the tickets, especially the return flight, I was not really thinking all that clearly. Brooke was in the middle of post-season play for her high school softball team. I did not really think in a million years that they would make it past the district games. They had not been playing that well in the weeks leading up to the tournament. As the days wore on, though, they kept winning games, and I soon realized that our return flight might be right in the middle of the regional championship game. Brooke could not miss the game, and certainly could not miss the homecoming welcome of her only brother. I stressed about the predicament I had gotten myself into.

Kelsey was also wrapping up the spring semester of her sophomore year at Samford University. We had to coordinate with her finals schedule to make sure she would be finished and at home before her brother arrived. We had been praying for Marvin to come home as soon as possible, but as we look back we realized God's timing was perfect. Kelsey and Brooke would be finished with their classes and have the entire summer to bond with their brother. I love how God sometimes shows you only a few steps ahead, not the entire staircase. He wants us to trust Him—that He knows best—but I admit that at times it was hard to trust during the process.

There were some last-minute items that I needed to gather before Marvin came home. I did not know exactly what size clothing he wore, so I planned on bringing a few different sizes with me for his return home. I really had no clue what size shoe he wore. The last time I was there was August 2013, I had traced an outline of his foot onto a piece of paper. As we all know, though, children's feet grow rapidly in the early years. I brought some new shoes with us, but, unfortunately, they were all way too big. Thankfully, Marvin did not mind being carried, or he probably would have been tripping all over the place. I prepared his room and made some "toddler proofing" changes to the house. I was not sure if he would have any interest in the items under the kitchen sink, or the knives in the kitchen drawer, but I wanted to make sure he was safe from the things he had probably never seen before.

I installed his car seats in my SUV and Mike's truck and drove around for several weeks with an empty car seat. I just kept envisioning all the fun conversations we were going to have. I imagined all the firsts he was going to experience, including riding in a car seat. Was he going to refuse to ride in one? From what I had seen of his personality, I did not think so, but you never know. He always loved riding in a vehicle in Haiti. He could sit there for hours, just taking in all the sights and sounds. I imagine anyone would, if they were cooped up day in and day out with no place to go. In America, our kids are reluctant to take long rides because they are riding in vehicles from the time they are born. Children adopted from orphanages seem to take pleasure in the everyday mundane things that we take for granted.

The days leading up to his homecoming flew by with travel preparations, packing, preparing his room and belongings, softball games, end-of-school-year craziness, and more. Our business was doing well, and the days passed quickly. The day we had waited on for over two years had finally come!

CHAPTER 15

Bringing Marvin Home

Every good and perfect gift is from above, coming down from the Father of the heavenly lights, who does not change like shifting shadows.
—JAMES 1:17

Mike and I were finally leaving on Wednesday to pick up our son and bring him home forever. We prayed that we would not encounter any hurdles in Haiti, but we were aware of the fact that these things often did not go as planned. We met up with our friends in the Knoxville airport and headed toward Haiti through Fort Lauderdale. We could all feel the excitement in the air. Travel went smoothly, and we landed in Port-au-Prince on time. Several days before our trip, we had communicated to Ricardo that we would be staying at the guest house in Port-au-Prince, as we had on many other trips. Ricardo was not geared up for guests at his guest house, and we much preferred to stay with people we knew rather than in a hotel. We also thought we had communicated that the kids could stay with us in Port-au-Prince at the guest house, so we assumed the kids would be waiting for us at the airport.

As we exited the airport, we quickly spotted Jameson waiting for us. It was so good to see him, and we gave hugs all around. He ushered us toward the parked utility truck where we were expecting to see the kids. When we saw they were not there, we were deflated to say the least. Where were the kids? We quickly asked Jameson as to their whereabouts, and he informed us they were in Camatin at the orphanage. We wondered how this was going to work. Were we staying the night in Camatin instead? We knew how far it was to the orphanage, and it was already late afternoon. Surely, we weren't going there and back in the same day. Jameson hopped on the phone, and I assumed he was calling Ricardo. Next thing you know, he said, "Okay, we go to Camatin." I was excited we were going, but very nervous at the same time. We asked if we were staying the night at the orphanage, and he said no. We all mentally prepared for the fact that we would be traveling back to Port-au-Prince at night, knowing how dangerous this would be.

Ricardo had made it very clear that all the adoptive children were to have a final goodbye with their birth parents, if they were still living. We knew this, and of course we wanted this to happen. It was not a big issue for us, because Roselina lived in Port-au-Prince, but the other families' birth parents lived near the orphanage in Camatin. We assumed they would be there at the orphanage to say their final goodbyes, but it would be dark when they returned home. This was not going at all as we had planned.

When I said that Jameson picked us up in a utility truck, I must describe what this truck was like. It was similar to a flatbed truck that had a cage over the bed area. Wooden benches had been added around the perimeter for people to sit on and the floor was finished in rough boards as well. We piled into the utility truck and headed toward the orphanage in Camatin. This required us to drive through Port-au-Prince and outlying areas during rush hour. We were not surprised when we hit major traffic on the other side of town. Though this was my seventh trip to Haiti, I had never experienced traffic this bad! We sat for hours in the same spot, in an area called Carrefour. We were literally inching along for hours. People had rushed to get ahead and created a bottleneck that could not be relieved. The UN and Haitian police were waving large machine guns, forcefully requiring vehicles to back up in order to get traffic flowing again.

About two hours into our nightmare traffic jam, we heard some very loud music ahead. Jameson stuck his head around to the back of the truck and told us to put our suitcases and bags underneath the wooden benches and to guard our things. We wondered what was coming up ahead. The music proceeded to get louder and louder, as people started parading past our vehicle singing and dancing. The next thing we knew, a huge party cage on wheels was passing by us. The music level was deafening. People were dancing on the vehicle and parading alongside it. Thankfully, it passed without incident, and Jameson informed us it was similar to a carnival celebration.

When we started our drive to Chante Lajwa, I had contacted Pastor Charles at the guest house to let him know that we would be arriving very late that night. His wife later told me that she prayed continually for our safety that evening. As the hours wore on, I calculated the time we could possibly be arriving back in Port-au-Prince, and it made me very nervous. I was praying over our travels and safety the whole way up the mountain.

LATE NIGHT GOODBYES

When we arrived at the orphanage, many of the older children ran out to greet us. We immediately noticed Marvin was not there and correctly assumed he was asleep. By the time we arrived, it was after eight o'clock. The other set of birth parents were at the orphanage when we arrived. We split up from the other family as they visited with their girls and their birth family and headed to Marvin's room. When we entered, he was sound asleep on his bed. This was not at all how I pictured his last moments at the orphanage. I felt like we were whisking him away in the cover of darkness. We gazed at our sleeping son. Was he going to understand what was about to happen? Could he really say a proper goodbye after he had fallen asleep for the evening? We tried to gently wake him up, but he cried at first. Then, when he truly woke up, I got that amazing neck hug from the most precious boy in the world.

As Mike spent time with Marvin and some of the older children, I visited with the director of the orphanage. She had recently given birth to a beautiful girl, and I was able to see her chubby cheeks and adorable curly hair as she slept. She looked to be the epitome of health, a true blessing when so many children born into poverty are malnourished. Next, I went back downstairs to spend some time with Madeline. She had done such an outstanding job of caring for our son and, most importantly, of loving him. I knew this was going to be extremely difficult for both of them. Without that tight bond and love from her, Marvin would not be the well-adjusted, loving boy he is today.

I had purchased a beautiful cross-shaped locket for Madeline. I placed a photo of her and Marvin within the locket. I prayed that, in the future, she would lovingly look upon that small token of our appreciation and fondly remember the precious boy who loved her dearly. As he grows older, he probably will not remember Madeline, but I hope we will never let him forget how much she loved him. I asked Jameson to translate our sincere appreciation to her, how much we loved her and wanted to thank her.

Since it was getting late, we really needed to head back to Port-au-Prince. One of Marvin's good friends started to cry before we even left the boys' bedroom. Another younger friend was sound asleep, and again pangs of guilt hit me. He would wake up in the morning, and one of his best friends in the world would be gone. Thankfully, both boys would make their own journey home to Knoxville just a few months later.

We left the boys' bedroom and gathered at the entrance to the orphanage. All the older girls gathered to sing goodbye to Marvin and the two sisters. It was heart wrenching. I wondered how many of these girls, who were not in the process of being adopted, felt rejected or unworthy. Because of the changes in the adoption law, this orphanage and ministry had chosen not to pursue any further adoptions. I prayed for those precious hearts, that they would know their worth in the Lord and not feel left behind.

As they were singing, Madeline was holding Marvin in her arms. She was bawling, he was bawling, and I was bawling. It was a disaster. Thankfully, Mike was not bawling. I have always been able to count on him to hold it together when I needed it the most. This was not at all what I envisioned. I hoped she would someday forgive us for taking him like this. She knew this day would come, yet she poured her heart and soul into raising a boy who would never be hers. After the girls sang their goodbye song, I gathered Marvin in my arms, and we walked around the backside of the truck so I could try to calm him down. He held tight and sobbed his little heart out. At such a young age, I think he truly realized that this was goodbye to the only woman he had trusted and loved like a mommy.

HEARTBREAK AND JOY

After the goodbyes, we all piled back into the utility truck and headed down the mountain, or should I say, "careened" down the mountain. As I mentioned before, this was a very dangerous mountain in daylight. The only positive was, there was very little traffic on the mountain at night. We were in for the roller coaster ride of our lives as Jameson skillfully raced down the mountain to try to get us safely to the guest house as soon as possible. I prayed feverishly the whole way down. Thankfully, Marvin slept most of the way. Once we reached the city, the other mom and I sat on the floor of the truck to be as inconspicuous as possible. The men kept their backs to the cab of the truck to be low profile as well. I had called Pastor Charles as we left the orphanage to let him know we were finally on the way. I felt terrible for keeping them up so late.

When we finally arrived, it was after eleven o'clock. They had kindly saved dinner for us, and we all ate ravenously. We had not eaten since lunchtime. Marvin was eager to eat again and, as usual, cleaned his plate. We readied for bed, and Marvin slept in the girls' bunk room with me and the other mom and her two girls. Mike, and the other father, crashed in the boys' bunk room. We all were thankful for being one step closer to bringing our children home for good.

EXIT LETTER REQUIREMENT

The next morning, Jameson arrived again to take us to obtain our exit letters. The Haitian organization that processed the adoption was named Institut du Bien-Etra Social et de Recherches, or IBESR for short. In English, the name meant Institute of Social Well-Being and Research. IBESR required each family to obtain an exit letter that would accompany their giant package of documents they would be taking home with them. The exit letter basically was the final seal of approval from IBESR and allowed you to pass through immigration when leaving the country. When we booked our flights, we had forgotten about the exit letter requirement, which could sometimes take two to five days to receive once in country. We thought this was something Ricardo could be working on our behalf before we arrived, but we were mistaken.

We all piled into the truck and headed over to the agency. On the way, we picked up another adoptive family that was getting ready to bring their daughter home from the same orphanage. It was great to meet them and hear their story as well. Adoptive parents almost always have an instant camaraderie, and this short meeting was no exception.

The agency was in a very unassuming building, but it did have a pretty reception desk that no one was attending when we arrived. We walked into a small front office that contained two desks and nine chairs lining the opposite walls. We sat down, taking up almost all the available chairs. Jameson conversed with the lady behind the first desk. He pulled out three thick, legal-sized files and handed them to the lady. She proceeded to shuffle papers, look at some documents, ask Jameson questions, and leave the room. It was all very confusing since we did not speak the language. Jameson then informed us that she wanted copies of all our documents. We had each taken with us six copies of our important documents, three in French and three in English. I was not sure how to package them, so I had included them together...each English version attached to its corresponding French version and each pair stapled together then collated for all three copies. Of course, that was not how they wanted them presented. They wanted just the French versions together.

Here I was in a hard, plastic office chair, trying to separate stapled documents without damaging them and while keeping them in order. It was a disaster. Thankfully, Mike was entertaining Marvin while I wrestled with the paperwork. After handing the lady our papers, she spent more time shuffling and rearranging.

As on most of these trips, I forgot to wean myself off caffeine before I left. I was quite addicted to iced tea, which was just not something you find in Haiti, and I did not drink coffee. After we had been there for some time, I was nursing a massive caffeine-withdrawal headache. I asked Jameson if I could find a soda anywhere nearby. He sent a gentleman he knew out to get me a soda, and the man came back with two very cold, frosty bottles of soda. Somehow I forgot what happens when you open a mostly frozen bottle of soda. You guessed it, almost the entire soda exploded in my lap and on the floor of IBESR. I was mortified! I tried my best to clean it up with the diaper wipes that I had, but I was now soaked and sticky. Very thankfully, the papers were not still in my lap at the time!

After more time passed, the other dad and I were asked to go with Jameson to a back room to pay. I was not aware we had to pay for the exit letter document, but we were willing to pay almost anything to get Marvin home with us. We went through a maze of offices and hallways and ended up in a very crowded room with three desks and floor-to-ceiling case files. When I say floor to ceiling, I promise I am not exaggerating. I was in awe, and was shocked that our file ever made it out of there to begin with. I mean no disrespect to the agency, but they were seriously in need of more space and more case workers, and a computer system would have been heaven sent.

The dad and I paid around thirty US dollars each and received our handwritten paper receipts for payment. We then headed back to join the rest of our group. We waited in that room, trying to entertain the kids with what little we had, for what seemed like an eternity. However, I was not complaining, because somehow Jameson worked his magic and, with God's favor, we left there with signed exit letters in hand. We took a picture with the IBESR sign on our way out.

FINAL GOODBYE AT DELIVRANS MWEN

After our successful trip to IBESR, we were free to relax a little bit before dinner that evening at the guest house. We had been in contact with Pastor Odson and wanted to take Marvin back to the original orphanage, Delivrans Mwen, to say goodbye to his friends and his half-brother and half-sister. We were not very excited about seeing the madame of the orphanage, but it would be a necessary part of the process. Pastor Odson picked us up, and we made the short, rocky ride over to the orphanage.

This would be our first visit to the orphanage's new location, and the new home was infinitely better than the original. Due to the generosity of a couple in our church, the children had been moved to this home which contained a working kitchen, laundry area, actual bedrooms for all to share, a fairly secure wall and gate, and a nice open courtyard. As usual, the children were thrilled to see us, as well as Marvin. In the fourteen months since Marvin had left, there was a marked difference in his health compared to the other children.

When the madame saw Marvin, she grabbed him in a huge bear hug, and laid him backwards on her lap as she showered him with affection. I could see the fear in his eyes while this was happening. I wondered if he was worried that we might leave him there. I wished I could speak Creole to reassure him that was not the case. I did not want to let him out of my sight. The fear that this woman could do something to sabotage the adoption was still fresh in my mind, fourteen months later. I still did not trust her, but I was grateful for the care that she provided for Marvin during his early years. It is obvious, now that he has been home for several years, that he was taken care of to the best of their ability, and most of all, that he must have been loved well in all three of his living situations before he came home.

All of these puzzle pieces make up Marvin's story and have shaped who he is today. I truly believe, and am thankful to God, that he is a well-adjusted, loving, intelligent, and active little boy because he received the necessary love as an infant and toddler. He may not have had enough food to eat, or a real place to call home, but he must have been loved and his basic needs met. This was the reason his manman surrendered him to the orphanage when he was one, because she did not have the means to care for her precious child anymore. She made the ultimate sacrifice in love and gave him up to the care of others.

We enjoyed about an hour with all the children at the orphanage. Mike played an impromptu game of soccer with the boys in the courtyard, while I visited with some of the girls. This usually meant getting my hair painfully braided. Did I mention that I am very tender headed?

I was concerned about one of the older girls who was doubled over with back pain. After we left, I shared my concern with Pastor Odson that she might have a kidney infection and prayed they would take her to the clinic if she got worse. We said our goodbyes and hugged and kissed all the kids we had grown to love, knowing that this might be the last time we saw them for many years to come.

After returning to the guest house, we cleaned up and spent some time trying to FaceTime the girls. They were so excited to get our update about the exit letter and to see their little brother on video. He was active and already rough-housing with his Papi Mike. We ate a delicious Haitian meal, as always, and discovered Marvin was petrified of cats, as the house kittens came into the dining room hoping for some scraps. After dinner, we said our goodnights and tried to sleep. As Marvin fell fast asleep to the hum of the room full of oscillating fans, I lay awake for quite some time pondering the events of the last few days. I could just barely imagine what Mary, the mother of Jesus, experienced as she pondered in her heart what was said about her son. Eventually, I dozed off to sleep, and I am sure I dreamed of the moment we would walk on American soil and Marvin would instantly become a United States citizen.

The next morning, we felt the excitement in the air as we, and the other adoptive family, readied our children and headed to the airport. Marvin's manman had spent the night with us and would ride with us to the airport for one final goodbye. As we pulled up to the Port-au-Prince airport, we hopped out and grabbed our luggage. We hugged and kissed our Haitian friends goodbye, and I lingered as I hugged his manman. Marvin did not seem upset to be leaving his man-man, but he had been separated from her for almost three years at this point. I was saddened for her, as I could not imagine the pain and hurt that she suffered, in doing what she felt was the best for her youngest son. She did not cry, and we turned to leave.

Once we made it through security, we stood in line for customs. We had a giant stack of documents to show them, if requested, plus our exit letter we had received from IBESR the previous day. It was interesting that, as we proceeded

Marvin's manman and half-brother and half-sister

through customs, our officer kept our exit letter but gave all our other documents back to us. The other couple we were traveling with had their officer keep their exit letter plus a lot of their official documents. This caused them concern when we compared notes after making it through customs, but it did not prove to be an issue for either one of us. One thing we learned among other adoptive parents was that there was not a whole lot of consistency on the Haitian side of things. This could be attributed to a lack of communication ability, given their infrastructure. We breathed a huge sigh of relief as we were somberly allowed to exit customs. The only thing now that stood in our way was boarding the aircraft and getting through customs in the US.

While we were waiting in the terminal, Marvin wanted to share a sip of my coffee frappe, but he proceeded to suck down the remaining half. I thought to myself, this could be a fun flight with a toddler hyped up on coffee and sugar! After what seemed like an eternity, our flight finally began boarding. When the gate agent passed us through, I started to tear up and really had to hold it together. Mike was his usual cool self, but I could tell he was really excited we were finally at the end of this journey. This was it; we were actually heading home! Seven hundred, ninety-three days after we met our son, he was finally coming home. As I gazed out the window during takeoff and tears welled up again, all I could say out loud was, "Thank You, Lord!"

WHEELS UP!

Marvin loved the airplane ride. He barely made a peep as he enjoyed playing with his toys and feeling the motion of the plane. He loved showing Mike, his Papi, how the airplane food tray opened and closed. He watched intently as we lifted off in Haiti and the landscape became a distant view. We made sure Marvin had plenty of snacks, and before long he had settled in for a nap. Mike and I rested in the knowledge that we were almost home. We touched down in Fort Lauderdale and proceeded to the special area for new citizens. We once again retrieved our giant stack of documents, and what could have taken hours took less than thirty minutes. With the official stamp and paperwork needed in hand, we proceeded to retrieve our international luggage and recheck it for our domestic flight back to Knoxville.

While hanging out in the airport, we discovered that Marvin was not a fan of lunch meat, which holds true to this day (with the exception of salami, I think, because it resembles pepperoni). With no delays we flew to Charlotte and then boarded the last leg of our flight home to Knoxville, where our family and friends were waiting for us to return.

As I mentioned earlier, when we booked our flights to Haiti, Brooke's softball team had not been playing to the best of their ability. I booked our return flights for the same Friday as her softball team's potential sub-state tournament game. I did not think the team would make it past the required district games, so in my anxiousness to bring our son home, I booked our flight a day too soon. As luck would have it, the true potential of the softball team started to shine in the postseason tournament. They won district and regionals, and the sub-state final game was scheduled for the same Friday evening. There was no way we were going to let Brooke miss the airport homecoming celebration of her little brother or the sub-state game, so we had to devise a plan to make sure both could happen.

ARRIVING IN KNOXVILLE

Our flight was scheduled to land around 7:00 p.m., which would be too early for Brooke to make the airport celebration. We knew there was another flight into Knoxville around 9:20 p.m. that evening. Rather than pay the more than three-hundred-dollar change fees for the later flight, we decided that we would keep the earlier flight and simply hang out in the terminal until the nine o'clock flight landed and pretend we were arriving on that flight. Disclaimer: to all the friends to whom I did not tell the truth, I am sorry; please forgive me. You know I do not like to even tell a little white lie, and this one was tough.

The funniest part was, we assumed we could eat dinner at the Ruby Tuesdays at the airport while we waited. We figured this would take up at least an hour of time. Unfortunately, it closed at 7:00 p.m., along with every other store and restaurant in the terminal. Knoxville is a very small airport, and once that last flight took off, everything closed. So here we were, stuck with a non-English speaking toddler with no dinner and only a few toys, snacks, and some rocking chairs to play with, while we waited almost two and a half hours for "our flight" to land. Marvin handled it like a champ. After Brooke's ballgame was finished (which they won!), she and her friends quickly made it to the airport, just in time to see us exit down the arriving flight ramp. Thankfully, in Knoxville, there is a connecting ramp between the gates and security and baggage claim where you are allowed to wait for arriving passengers. It was the perfect place for family and friends to wait for our arrival.

Mike and Marvin waiting in the
Knoxville airport

Our amazing family and friends made the effort to be there for us as we arrived. They made posters, brought balloons, and were genuinely thrilled to see us, receiving us with open arms. All of them had prayed and believed for this special day. They will never know how much that meant to us.

As we came down the ramp, Kelsey and Brooke came forward to meet us. For the first time in our lives, we were a true family of five, and the girls had a little brother. It had been over a year since they had seen Marvin in person, but I could tell he recognized his sisters. During previous visits to Haiti, we had left behind laminated photos of his family, so he could keep them with his small set of possessions. After a long family hug, we turned to greet the rest of our family and friends. We received hugs all around and tried to tell the story of how things went when we picked him up. Marvin did great in this sea of English-speaking and strange-looking

Our amazing family and friends at the airport to welcome us home

people. He landed in the arms of a few friends but quickly made his way back to either me or Mike. A precious friend made a wonderful welcome home video, set with photos and music. We still watch that video today and look back with fondness at the memories of Marvin's homecoming day.

Some awesome friends took charge and gathered our luggage and even our car. We visited some more in the baggage claim area, and as it grew closer to ten o'clock, we loaded up our car and headed home. This was the first time Marvin had ever ridden in a car seat, and he seemed to like it. He was going to be our master traveler very soon, and thankfully he hit the ground running.

HOME SWEET HOME

We arrived home and began filling up the bathtub for Marvin. This would be his first warm bath ever. We were embarking on so many firsts. It was hard to imagine what his little mind was thinking about all his new experiences. As we lowered him into the bath, he happily played with some of the tub toys we had waiting for him. Do not laugh, but I did briefly consider not introducing him to the world of playing in the bathtub. In my mind, I thought about all the time I would save if we just continued with showers. Of course, my crazy notion of saving time was quickly replaced by the joy and laughter of a little one enjoying playtime in a warm bath. No, I would not rob him of this childhood pleasure.

Mike's sister, Buffy, and Kelsey and Brooke's best friends had come over to see us get him settled in. They were there as we showed Marvin his very own room and explained that it was all his. His eyes lit up in excitement. We also finally fed him a proper dinner, and he quickly cleaned his plate. As we would find out in the coming months and years, Marvin loves to eat, and eats all kinds of grown-up foods. He is one of the least picky eaters I know.

After kisses all around, we finally tucked our son into *his* bed, in *his* room, with *his* family just down the hall, if needed. The moment I had prayed and waited so long for was finally here! It is very difficult to describe the feeling of waiting to bring your adopted child home. It feels like the longest pregnancy of your life. It was difficult to keep the worry and fears at bay. You worry about all the milestones you are missing, all the possible things that could happen while you are apart, and of course, you mix in third-world-country worries as well. However, the Bible is very clear about worry. In my daily prayers for our son, I had to put my trust in the Lord, each and every day.

CHAPTER 16

Settling In

Trust in the LORD forever, for the LORD, the LORD himself, is the Rock eternal.
—ISAIAH 26:4

The first full day Marvin was home was spent playing and exploring. We all played on the trampoline, played with sidewalk chalk, played with toys, and ate! We even visited our favorite family-owned Mexican restaurant where the owners, our friends, had walked through this journey with us. They were thrilled to meet Marvin, and he proceeded to eat a full plate of chicken, rice, and beans. Some of the literature we read on adoption suggested that we stay at home and cocoon, so to speak. They recommended keeping the bond between the adopted child and only the immediate family, but we just felt that was not what Marvin needed to thrive.

I planned on taking the summer off and being there every step of the way for him. That summer, I was his mother *and* his playmate. One thing I had not anticipated was his fear of being alone, and his inability to self-play or self-entertain. Since he had lived in a group orphanage setting for most of his life, he had never been alone in a room by himself, ever! When he first came home, he would follow us around to whatever room we happened to be in. He would not stay in any room by himself. At night, he would sleep in his bed by himself, but I was pretty sure there was a lot of fear attached to that. We made it our goal to slay those fears, to help him feel safe and secure, and to help him learn how to use his imagination through self-play. It took him about a year to learn how to play by himself, but he finally learned how to sit and play a few imaginary games with his toys. To this day, he still seeks out people to play with, and I do not think that will ever change.

As I mentioned earlier, Brooke's softball team won that sub-state game on Friday night and was headed to the state championship. We certainly did not want to miss this once-in-a-lifetime opportunity for her. Her team had to take their final exams early, as they planned to leave Knoxville for middle Tennessee on Monday. I also had scheduled an adoption clinic medical appointment at Vanderbilt for the Monday after we returned home from Haiti. In my mind, it made perfect sense that we would pack up our adopted son after being home three days, and travel to Nashville first thing Monday morning. We knew we would most likely be there all week as they progressed in the tournament. Mike and Brooke traveled with the team, and Kelsey and I ventured off early with Marvin.

On Sunday, I had tested Marvin's tolerance for milk by giving him a few ounces to drink in the morning. He seemed to tolerate that well, so Monday morning I packed him a sippy cup full of milk as we hit the road. We made it about halfway to Nashville when Marvin looked miserable and said he needed to use the "twalet," which meant toilet. We got off at the next exit and pulled into a brand-new gas station and fast-food restaurant. I unbuckled his car seat and frantically rushed into the store to find a bathroom. Much to my shock, the woman behind the counter stated that their bathroom had been out of service for days.

As Marvin writhed in pain, I had to think fast about what we were going to do. He obviously was not going to make it to the next exit. I ran back to the car and grabbed the empty plastic container I brought with us to try to collect a stool sample for the adoption medical clinic. We swiftly ran around the corner, and I parked his little bum in the middle of the plastic container in the mulch bed. As he was releasing his bowels, he started sweating profusely and then went limp. So here I was squatting down to hold him in the seated position on the container, and he was passed out in my arms. Just then a nice stranger pulled into a nearby parking spot and asked if we were okay. I had to briefly explain the situation and thanked him for his help. I managed to clean Marvin up, secure our sample, and lay him over my shoulder. Kelsey was trying to help, but the smell was overwhelming, and she backed away to keep from losing her breakfast. We finally laid him back into his car seat, sound asleep, and continued our journey to Nashville.

He had passed out after eating once before while I was in Haiti. As we would later find out through testing, Marvin had giardia, an intestinal parasite that was very common for third-world adoptees. When you have giardia for a long period, it can flatten the villi of your intestines and cause diarrhea, intestinal cramping, and lactose intolerance. In feeding him milk, I unwittingly gave Marvin the very thing that would make him violently ill. Thankfully, we were prescribed a course of medicine for the parasite, and all follow-up testing came back clear. I must insert that he was the best little medicine taker, too. The liquid medicine he needed to take had to be compounded by a pharmacist, and I had heard the taste was atrocious, but he took every dose with nary a complaint. The lactose intolerance cleared up within six months of being home.

MEDICAL TESTS AND SOFTBALL

Kelsey, Marvin, and I arrived safely at Vanderbilt Hospital, checked in, and were sitting in the waiting area. While I ran to the restroom, the nurse came to take us to our room. She assumed Kelsey was his mom and I was the grandma, so she told Kelsey she would let "Grandma" know which room we were in. Flustered, she explained that she was the sister and, at nineteen years of age, was not the mom. When Kelsey told me this, we both had a good laugh as I had gone from being the "young" mom when she and Brooke were little to the "old" mom now! This would not be the last time it happened, but thankfully, for my ego's sake, it doesn't happen too often.

During our appointment with the doctor, I explained what had happened on the way over. Marvin was now awake but was very subdued as he was put through a battery of tests. After the physical exam, it was time for blood work. We went to the phlebotomist to get at least four vials of blood drawn. This large, gruff woman proceeded to harshly stick Marvin's vein. Marvin cried hard, but he was such a trooper, and kept his arm very still. The worst part was yet to come. After three vials that vein quit producing, or blew out, so she had to stick him again. Kelsey and I were fuming as she dug and fished for a new vein. Poor Marvin screamed and cried, almost like a howl, but he bravely kept his arm still. I have never in my life wanted to smack a healthcare worker, but I will tell you the urge was strong. We thanked God when it was all over, and Marvin was passed out on my shoulder once again. Thankfully, Marvin's medical tests came back with only a few minor issues that we were able to resolve within a few months of coming home. This was a blessing I hope we never take for granted. He was extremely healthy, considering his background.

We had scheduled a psychological appointment following the medical appointment, so Kelsey and I gathered up all of our things and headed down the hall. I was glad we had this appointment because the doctor had some useful tips and insights, but I was not sure I got my money's worth because Marvin slept through the entire appointment. One piece of advice we walked away with was to let him be a baby for a while. She said if he wanted to be carried everywhere, we should carry him. If he wanted to snuggle, let him. Basically, we should allow him to "relive" some of his missed early childhood so that he would feel safe, secure, and attached.

After this appointment, we headed to our hotel in Murfreesboro for the softball state tournament. Over the next few days, we visited the Nashville Zoo, played on huge playgrounds, watched softball games, ate lots of food, and met our extended softball family. Some of the younger girls from the team immediately bonded with Marvin, and he loved playing with them. Mike's parents were staying there as well, and I know they enjoyed getting to know their new grandson. I loved seeing his facial expressions and hearing his giggles as we slid down a giant slide for the first time. We celebrated all of the late May birthdays, which included Brooke, Mike, and Kelsey, as well as our twenty-first wedding anniversary, while we were there.

After five days of games, the team walked away as the state runner up. We were so proud of this team and all they had accomplished. In one short week, Marvin had become an official softball "little brother," complete with many trips to the concession stand and ballpark playground. This tournament would be the beginning of many years of spoiling by the sweetest softball families. Marvin was treated in such a special way. We will never forget those precious first years.

HIT THE GROUND RUNNING

In typical fashion for our family, we had scheduled Brooke's sixteenth birthday party for the weekend following Marvin's arrival and at the end of their softball games in Murfreesboro. We had rented a friend's summer camp for the night, which included a gymnastics facility, ropes climbing course, tubing, and sand volleyball. On Friday after the softball games, we drove back to Knoxville, loaded up everything we needed for the party, and headed back out with vehicles full of friends to celebrate Brooke's big milestone! Marvin had a blast running all around the camp. He especially loved the trampolines and foam pit.

I pretty much took the rest of the summer off from work, thanks to my wonderful office manager. Another gift in the timing of everything was that Kelsey was home from college for the summer, so we were able to bond as a family of five. We purchased season passes to Dollywood amusement park. Marvin rode the kid-friendly roller coaster twice that summer but then decided it was a little too scary. We traveled to Kentucky to gather with my side of the family and introduce Marvin to everyone. He became fast friends with all of his cousins, and they were so sweet to spend so much time playing with him. He loved riding in a boat and on an inner tube. We discovered he was quite the daredevil. He learned to ride his bike, ride a scooter, jump on the trampoline, and hit a baseball. Mike enjoyed teaching his son so many new things, especially swimming. Marvin took to the water like a fish and was easily swimming by the end of the summer.

Because he was so used to spending every waking hour with other children, I enrolled him in a church preschool two days a week, which he started mid-summer. His teachers were wonderful and helped him get acclimated, despite the language barrier. I made a little language "cheat sheet" to help them with the basic commands they would need him to know. He loved spending this time with other children, and language was seldom a barrier.

His language quickly developed, and within seven weeks it was like a lightbulb went off and he completely switched over to English. They said it would happen fast, but it was amazing to see it happen seemingly overnight. We still have contact with his manman, so I was sad and shocked at how quickly he lost the ability to speak Creole. I just assumed the Creole would stick around longer than it did. Within three months he could not even speak basic Creole words. If I prompted him, to jog his memory on a particular Creole word, he would mispronounce it. The human brain is a mystery. I did my best to translate for them when she did call, and thankfully through an app, we could send pictures and videos and translate text messages into Creole, and vice versa. About eight months after he came home, Marvin switched from calling Mike "Papi" to "Daddy." I was kind of hoping he would keep the Papi forever.

Marvin was funny about our modest house. It took about three months before he would agree that our house was his house. The orphanage was a huge house with many bedrooms, huge bathroom areas, a big open courtyard inside, and tons of land. In Marvin's words the orphanage, or his house, was "gwo" or "big," and our house was "piti" or "small." Thankfully, he finally embraced his new, reduced living quarters.

THRIVING ALL AROUND

Marvin was thriving as a joyful, healthy, well-adjusted little boy. He was quickly catching up to his peers in size and knowledge. When he first came home, he weighed only thirty-five pounds, but he soon gained weight and grew stronger. He started kindergarten shortly after turning five years old. He needed speech services to help with stuttering that had developed when he switched from Creole to English. We figured the school was the best place to get those services and the extra help he would need academically. Thankfully, by the time he reached second grade he had caught up with his peers in all areas and is now a solid A/B student. He graduated speech services by fourth grade, and most people could never detect that he had issues with stuttering. The Lord had placed the absolute perfect teachers and coaches in his life, to nurture his growth in the best way possible. We will be forever grateful to those amazing people who have loved our Marvin along the way.

According to his early grade schoolteachers, he had a love for math and taking tests. He is great with numbers, so I may finally have someone follow in my engineering footsteps. He easily makes new friends and is often the life of the party. He is boisterous, active, and all boy. I like to say that he is "full on" unless he is sleeping. He loves to go places and do things and has often been upset if we just stay at home. He likes to know where we are going and what we are doing for each day. He loves ninjas, swimming, soccer, rough housing, and bedtime stories. If it were not for the color of his skin, you would never know he was not our biological child. He is the perfect fit for our family in every way.

Epilogue

" 'Love the Lord your God with all your heart and with all your soul and with all your mind and with all your strength.' The second is this: 'Love your neighbor as yourself.' There is no commandment greater than these."
—MARK 12:30,31

Some days our fifty years of age feels old as we continue this parenting journey 2.0, but we would not change a thing. Are some days hard and discouraging as we approach the middle school years? Of course, but we will never forget the gift and responsibility we have been given. Raising any child is hard and will always have its ups and downs. However, Marvin is the biggest blessing we never knew we needed.

He has become quite a leader and has given his life to Christ and been baptized. It is encouraging to hear teachers, coaches, and church leaders recognize the unique gifts God has placed in him. He has a strong Haitian personality (we often say he is the loudest child ever) but the most tender heart within. He has a passion and a love for people. We often call him the Pied Piper as younger children seem to flock to him. We still cannot wait to see the big things God has in store for our little buddy, who is not so little anymore.

Pretty soon he will be towering over all four of us, but it will still be our job to guide him successfully into adulthood. We pray he will always put Christ first and let the Lord light his path as he navigates this world. It really boils down to two things: love God and love people. If we instill those values into our son, God will take care of the rest.

We want to say a final thank you to the many people who crossed our paths and made this journey possible. You know who you are, and we hope you know how much you mean to us. We pray this book always keeps your sacrifice of time and effort at the forefront of Marvin's story. Be blessed—we love you!

SOME OF OUR FIRST-YEAR MEMORIES

Kelsey & Marvin, his first week home, cheering on Brooke at her games

The Wyrosdick family at our church's welcome home reception: Aunt B (Buffy), Mike, Kelsey, Brooke, Marvin, Katie, Big Papi (Jay) & Granny (Sam)

*Katie's family, Grandpa Charlie and
Grandma Lucy, at their first visit*

*Marvin's first visit with Grandpa
(Bob) (Katie's stepdad)*

Celebrating his first Christmas with Katie's family:
Cousin Nick, Mike, Grandma (Lucy), Grandpa (Charlie),
Cousin Jack, Aunt Amy, Uncle Steve
2nd row: Brooke, Marvin, Kelsey, Katie

Appendix

"The King will reply, 'Truly I tell you, whatever you did for one of the least of these brothers and sisters of mine, you did for me.'"
—MATTHEW 25:40

I would like to suggest some resources for those considering adoption. If that's you, my first and biggest advice would be to pray, pray, and pray. This will be an extremely difficult yet rewarding journey. I could never had made it without my faith.

Some children suffer from what is called Reactive Attachment Disorder (RAD), and I would encourage you to do extensive research about this disorder. You need as many tools in the toolbox as possible when your child comes home. It is important to learn all you can about your future child's early years. Was he nursed, loved, cared for, and held as a baby, or was he neglected, starved, abused? Knowing the answer to these questions will better prepare you for the battle ahead. If the child was neglected or abused in any way, it will be a battle and you need to be prepared. I also want you to know that sometimes it does not turn out the way you had hoped or dreamed, and that's okay too. God can redeem even the darkest of days and disappointments, in His time and in His way. We may not see the end plan with our eyes, but you can be assured that God does.

The financial burden of adoption, especially international adoption, is a challenge as well. Some funding options include fundraisers, home equity loans, non-profit resources, family, and more. For us, we did a combination of equity and family. We look back on those days and we are not sure how God worked it out financially, but praise God, He did! Each and every bill we ever had was paid in a timely manner. I would also encourage adoption through foster care. There is a huge need in our country for forever homes for children in foster care, and this is often a more affordable option for families.

RECOMMENDED ADOPTION RESOURCES

- Show Hope: Their cornerstone work is adoption aid grants. They also provide practical help including an annual "Hope for the Journey Conference." They provide links to professional resources to help come alongside you in your time of need. *showhope.org*

- How to Adopt: Show Hope also sponsors the "How to Adopt" website, which is a wealth of knowledge including first steps, understanding the process, and pre+post adoption support. *howtoadopt.org*

- US Government resources: *childwelfare.gov/topics/adoption* & *childwelfare.gov/topics/outofhome/foster-care/fam-foster*

RECOMMENDED READING

- *Successful Adoption: A Guide for Christian Families* by Natalie Gillespie (Thomas Nelson)

- *The Connected Child: Bring Hope and Healing to Your Adoptive Family* by Karyn Purvis, David Cross, and Wendy Lyons Sunshine (McGraw Hill)

- *The Connected Parent: Real-Life Strategies for Building Trust and Attachment* by Karyn Purvis and Lisa Qualls (Harvest House Publishers)

- *Parenting Children of Trauma: The Foster-Adoption Guide to Understanding Attachment Disorder* by Marcy Pusey (Miramare Ponte Press)

- If your adoption will be transracial, I suggest finding resources specific to transracial adoptions as well. We read *I'm Chocolate, You're Vanilla: Raising Healthy Black and Biracial Children in a Race-Conscious World* by Marguerite Wright (Jossey-Bass).

Acknowledgments

My Lord and Savior, Jesus Christ: Thank You for the gift of my husband, Mike, daughters, Kelsey and Brooke, and son, Marvin. They are my greatest joy and blessing, and I owe it all to You! Thirty years ago, I could have never imagined the life You have given me. If someone told me we would be adopting internationally, I would have thought they were crazy. Thank You for instilling in me an early love for children during my days as a YMCA camp counselor and day-care worker.

Mike: Thank you for being a willing "partner in crime" in this life. I love that you make me laugh daily and always keep me on my toes. Thank you for loving me when I am hard to love, for being the calm in the storm, and for being the opposite to my "worst-case scenario" brain. Thank you for being one of the best dads there is to our children. You have helped raise two incredible young women who have figured out this "adulting" thing pretty well. It is a joy and warms my heart when I see you and Marvin together. At times, I cringe when you two rough-house, but that appears to be exactly what God designed for boys. I am so thankful he has your footsteps to follow, and am just praying he will not inherit your nickname: "Stitch"!

Kelsey and Brooke: To say we are proud of you just does not adequately express our feelings. First, you both made it through high school and college with a deep love for the Lord and your faith in Him intact. That is really an accomplishment in a day and time when the world tries so hard to pull you away. Second, thank you for being willing to serve in Haiti and for opening your heart to a little brother, regardless of the changes to our family dynamic. We know you adore your little brother even when he is being a stinker and wants to have Mom and Dad's attention all to himself. Third, thanks to both of you for always being an extra set of eyes and hands when I need your help. I love how Marvin treats you both exactly like you were his biological sisters with the constant joking and teasing. It is obvious God chose him to be your brother, and the strong bond you will always share is a gift to be treasured.

Family and friends: Thank you very much for all your prayers, gifts, love, and financial support. You probably thought we were crazy, but you never voiced your concerns and just supported us all the way. Thank you for taking care of Brooke when we were out of the country, for hosting an amazing adoption shower, for being there when we landed in the Knoxville airport, for encouraging me to write this book, and most of all for loving us and loving Marvin as if he were one of your own.

To our Adoption Angels: Thank you to those dear friends in Haiti, and at home, who helped make this adoption possible. Thank you for the late-night phone calls, emails, and trips to Haiti on our behalf. Thank you for spending your own money on essentials, and for saying yes when the easy thing would have been to say no. Thank you for opening your home in Haiti and your heart to a precious little boy who needed a forever family. Thank you for believing in us and in God's plan.

Faith Promise Church: We are extremely grateful to our church and your heart for missions. Thank you for walking alongside us during the process, allowing us to tag along on mission trips and accomplish adoption tasks while under your prayers and protection of a group, and most of all for loving Marvin the minute he came home. Thank you for partnering with us in bringing him up in the way he should go. We could not do this without you.

Traci: God blessed me with some of the most amazing extended family members when I married Mike, and you are one of my greatest treasures. Your faith is as deep as anyone I know, and I pray each time we are together that just a little bit of that deepness rubs off on me. I cannot thank you enough for editing my book, not once, but twice in the midst of your crazy schedule. I will forever be grateful for your sacrifice of time, guidance, and prayers through this process.

Lynn: My editor and publisher extraordinaire. Thank you for your time, guidance, and sound advice. I am so grateful our paths crossed on this project. You are a blessing, and maybe we can do it again on the next adventure: *Growing Up Marvin*???

Marvin: I hope you know how much you are loved and treasured and pray that your written story becomes a cherished link between your current world and your past life in Haiti. God has ordered your days and I pray you always stay plugged into the heart of Jesus where you find His love and peace that surpasses all understanding. I pray, someday, you will get to visit your homeland and meet some of the amazing people who made your journey possible. We are blessed by your infectious laugh, tender heart, constant conversation, and *big* personality. We are so proud of the young man you are becoming and love you so much.